STUDY TACTICS

William H. Armstrong
Winner of the National School Bell Award
for distinguished interpretation in the
field of education and author of the
Newbery Medal award-winning book, *Sounder.*

and

M. Willard Lampe II
Chairman, Department of General Studies
Master, Greek and Latin
Kent School, Kent, Connecticut

BARRON'S

Barron's Educational Series, Inc.
Woodbury, N.Y. • London • Toronto • Sydney

All inquiries should be addressed to:
Barron's Educational Series, Inc.
113 Crossways Park Drive
Woodbury, New York 11797

International Standard Book No. 0-8120-2590-3

Library of Congress Catalog Card No. 83-15345

Library of Congress Cataloging in Publication Data
Armstrong, William Howard, 1914–
  Study tactics.

  Also published under title: Study tips.
  Includes bibliographical references.
  1. Study, Method of. I. Lampe, M. Willard.
II. Title.
LB1049.A72 1983b   371.3'028'12   83-15345
ISBN 0-8120-2590-3 (pbk.)

PRINTED IN THE UNITED STATES OF AMERICA
3 4 5 6 7 800 9 8 7 6 5 4 3 2 1

CONTENTS

Preface   **ix**

1. Introduction: From These Roots   1

   The Gift of Perception   1
   The Gift of Thought   2
   The Gift of Communication   3

2. Listening: The Easy Way to Learn   7

   True Confessions   7
   The Most Difficult of All Learning Processes   8
   The Problem of Coordination   8
   The Problem of Speaking Rate   9
   Learning to Follow the Leader   9
   The Problem of Working on Your Own   10
   Few Do but Many Can   11
   The Classroom a Proving Ground   12
   Taking Notes: The Ultimate Key to Success   13
   Listening Aids   15
   Listening Errors to Avoid   17
   Daily Exercises in Listening   18
   Looking Back   19

3. The Classroom: Atmosphere for Achievement   21

   True Confessions   21
   Important Elements of Classroom Success   21
   Partnership with the Teacher   22
   The Influence of the Teacher   23
   The Way to "Use" the Teacher   24
   Hints on Attitude   24
   What Kind of Student Are You?   26
   Developing Confidence in Your Abilities   27
   Looking Back   30

4. Study Time: Design for Success   31

   True Confessions   31
   Time Is Learning's Most Important Tool   31

Finding Where the Hours Go ... 32
Busy, but Well Organized ... 35
Making Your Schedule Work ... 40
Looking Back ... 42

5. Mastering Assignments: Methods of Study ... 43

True Confessions ... 43
Difference Between Reading and Studying ... 44
Study Methods ... 44
Making Good Study Methods Work ... 50
Looking Back ... 53

6. Note-Taking: Summaries, Outlines, Maps ... 55

True Confessions ... 55
Kinds of Notes ... 55
Format ... 56
The Making of a Good Summary ... 56
Finding Models of Condensing ... 58
The Art of Outlining ... 60
Individual Methods of Condensing ... 65
Mapping ... 66
Suggestions for Better Summary Writing ... 73
Suggestions for Better Outlines ... 74
Suggestions for Better Mapping ... 75
Looking Back ... 76

7. Spelling and Punctuation: Hallmarks of Excellence ... 79

True Confessions ... 79
Hallmarks of Quality ... 80
General Spelling Faults and How to Correct Them ... 80
Syllables and Sound in Correct Spelling ... 83
Spelling Rules and Exceptions ... 85
Spelling Demons ... 87
Summary of Practices for Spelling Mastery ... 91
The Function of Punctuation ... 92
The Characteristics of the Marks of Punctuation ... 93
Summary of Enlightened Punctuation ... 94
Looking Back ... 95

8. Studying for Subjects: Adapting Your Methods to the
    Subject   97

    True Confessions   97
    Method Plus Work Equals Success   98
    Foreign Languages   98
    English   101
    History   106
    Mathematics   112
    Science   115
    A Final Word   118
    Looking Back   118

9. A Feeling for School Subjects: It Grows from Interest   121

    True Confessions   121
    The Beginning of Success Is Interest   122
    Try Interest Instead of Prejudice for Languages   123
    Try Smiles for Mathematics Instead of Frowns   126
    Studying Science   130
    History—Enjoy What You Cannot Avoid   133
    English Gives Meaning to Feeling   136
    Looking Back   136

10. Reading: Faster with More Understanding   139

    True Confessions   139
    The Nature of Reading   140
    Understanding More   145
    Reading Faster   150
    Practices for Better Reading   152
    Looking Back   153

11. Words: How to Improve Your Knowledge of Them   155

    True Confessions   155
    Why Study Words?   156
    The Many Qualities of Words   156
    The Origin of Words   157
    The Excitement of Words   158
    Practices for Vocabulary Improvement   165
    Looking Back   167

12. Written Work: The Product and Its Package 169

True Confessions 169
The Nature of the Product 170
Writing Regular Themes 172
Four Steps in Theme Writing 173
The Nature of the Package 178
Improving Your Writing 180
How to Judge Quality 183
Suggestions for Improving Written Work 183
Looking Back 184

13. Written Work: Style and Usage 187

True Confessions 187
Models of Good Style 188
Clarity 191
Simplicity 195
Choosing Active Words 196
Sincerity 197
Order 198
Selection of Best Words 198
Common Usage Errors 200
Looking Back 208

14. Research Papers: Steps to Success 211

True Confessions 211
What Is a Research Paper 211
The Nine Steps in Research 212
Proceeding to Do Research 216
Footnotes and Bibliography 218
A Word of Caution 222
Practices for Better Research Papers 223
Looking Back 223

15. The Library: How to Use It 225

True Confessions 225
How to Find a Book 225
Systems of Classification 228

Reference Books   232
Records and Films   235
Practices for Better Library Use   236
Looking Back   237

16. Tests and Examinations: The Big Score   239

True Confessions   239
The Nature of Tests to Come   240
Attitude: The First Step   241
Learning from Tests   243
Reviewing for Tests and Examinations   244
Suggestions for Successful Review   246
Taking Tests and Examinations   248
Summary of Rules for Reviewing For and Taking Tests
   and Examinations   253
Looking Back   254

17. Motivation: Each Must Find It for Oneself   257

The Reach and the Grasp   257
Motivation—Imperishable   261
Motivation—A Seed Falling upon Good Ground   263

PREFACE

This book is a guide to assist you in developing quality in your work as a student. It explains techniques that will enable you to work effectively and efficiently. There are suggestions to help you use your time properly, improve your listening ability, broaden your knowledge of words, take notes skillfully, master the course content in as little time as possible, study for and take tests, find information swiftly, and submit better written assignments.

In short, this book is designed to help you learn how to learn, to acquire a feeling for learning, and to understand the importance of the things you study.

INTRODUCTION: FROM THESE ROOTS

Learning is not an easy task. It has never been one, and it never will be, despite the fond hopes of generations of students. Comprising *perception, thought,* and *communication,* learning involves too much to be easy. These wonderful gifts of perception, thought, and communication are your natural endowment. How you use them will determine to a great degree how successful you are as a student and a learner.

The Gift of Perception

Perception is the gift that enables you to become acquainted with the world around you. History offers illustrations of men who used their perceptive powers to achieve success. The story of Joseph in the Book of Genesis is one of the world's greatest success stories. Joseph was a slave and a prisoner in the stone quarries, an alien—completely alone in a strange land and numbered among the dead by his kinsmen. His chance audience with the Pharaoh came because Joseph had a reputation as a dreamer and an interpreter of dreams. But Joseph was more than a dreamer. Had it not been for keen perception, Joseph might well have been taken back to the stone quarries after he had interpreted the Pharaoh's dream to mean seven years of plenty followed by seven years of famine. Joseph gave purpose to what he had perceived by suggesting that the Pharaoh prepare for the famine by storing grain during the years of plenty. The Pharaoh made Joseph his second-in-command and put him in charge of the whole program of preparation for the years of famine. Joseph saw with his eyes and his mind, and acted upon the purpose he had visualized. This is keen perception—perception that sees through to the end.

There is a wonderful story of a boy who arrived at a newspaper office in response to a help wanted advertisement. Much to his dismay there were twenty-two boys ahead of him in line. A keen sense of perception solved the problem that confronted him. He wrote on the back of an envelope: "Dear Sir, I am twenty-third in line. Please do not hire anyone until you have talked to me." He then folded the envelope and asked the person in front of him to pass it forward to the person doing the interviewing. The interviewer read the note and continued to speak with each applicant, but the boy twenty-third in line got the job, because of his sharp perceptive sense.

An amusing and true story may perhaps alert you to a state of constant watchfulness for putting this gift of perception to work. Five days before examination time, a French teacher filled the classroom blackboard with material—verbs, sentences in English, sentences in French, lists of words. He taught a total of sixty students; daily, they sat in his classroom for five days. When the examination was passed out, there was a loud chorus of groans. Where had they seen this before?—it had been on the blackboard for five days. Two people out of sixty had used their keen perceptive powers. They made perfect scores; the other fifty-eight made generally what the teacher had expected—the level of achievement they had made during the term. Perception is the gift that acquaints you with the world around you. It is a precious gift. Use it fully, constantly, and wisely. Be sure you are seeing when you look.

The Gift of Thought

Perception without thought brings neither conscious purpose nor action. The gift of thought is the one without which all other gifts would lie dormant. Your whole education is designed to bring growth to your ability to think. If this were not so, the number of puzzles that increase with each year of your life would overwhelm you.

The gift of thought provides the human mind with the capacity to deal in abstractions. A sound, for example, is an abstraction that can be converted into deep feeling. It can also be made into a symbol—a spoken word. Man has the further ability to record the spoken word by writing and make it into something visible. The gift of thought makes possible all the valuable things that make our world: material things, ranging from the first flint-hatchet of the cave man to the most advanced rocket; and im-material things—religion and morals, institutions such as home and community, and qualities and standards.

The Gift of Communication

Let us quote from Dr. Albert Einstein's book, *The World as I See It*:

> Only the individual can think, and thereby create new values for society—nay, even set up new moral standards to which the life of the community conforms. Without creative, independently thinking and judging personalities, the upward development of society is as unthinkable as the development of the individual personality without the nourishing soil of the community.[1]

Communication and community come from the same root word, and without the ability to communicate, the community would be impossible. Through the gift of communication you will receive your education, and the extent to which you develop the ability to communicate with others will help to determine the success or failure of your life. The memory of mankind—its total knowledge and beliefs—is communicated to you through the medium of language.

1.   Albert Einstein, *The World As I See It* (Princeton: Princeton Univ. Press, 1949), 84.

Winston Churchill was one of the world's great masters at the art of communication. It was his ability to communicate that stirred the British first, and then the world, into action against Hitler. An American correspondent cabled in one story: "Winston Churchill has mobilized the English language and sent it into battle." Indeed, he had done just that—and he won. When he became prime minister in England's "darkest hour," he communicated to his people what they knew, but feared to utter: "I have nothing to offer but blood and toil, tears and sweat." When Belgium had surrendered, France fallen, and the German army stood on the French coast and stared menacingly across at the white cliffs of Dover, Churchill communicated to his countrymen the defiant and resolute feeling that needed to be given voice:

> We shall defend our island, whatever the cost may be. We shall fight on the beaches. We shall fight on the landing grounds. We shall fight on the fields and in the streets. We shall fight in the hills. We shall never surrender. Let us brace ourselves to our duties, and so bear ourselves that, if the British Empire and Commonwealth last for a thousand years, men will say: This was their finest hour.[2]

It is well within the confines of reason to say that this one man did more than any other single man to win World War II. The world may never require of you such exertion of your gift of communication, but you must never cease working to increase the power of this great gift. In high school and college, the degree of success you attain in communicating what you have learned will constitute your teachers' sole means of grading your work— both oral and written.

Perception, thought, and communication—these make possible the memory of the past, provide the vision and dream of the future—these are the chief ingredients of learning, the basic reasons for education.

---

2.   Winston Churchill, *The Second World War*, 6 vols., (Boston: Houghton Mifflin Co., 1949), 2:25.

The three gifts of perception, thought, and communication, when combined with the willingness to work hard, provide the basic ingredients of success in learning. By employing these factors, a student will be able to make his studying count for something and be both effective and efficient.

LISTENING: THE EASY WAY TO LEARN

True Confessions

"I never remember the names of people who are introduced to me."

"I didn't get what you said because I was thinking of how to phrase my own comment."

"I forgot the due date for the book report. Did Mrs. Benson tell us when it had to be handed in?"

If these quotations are familiar, you need not despair. You can console yourself that you are one among many. You have forgotten, as have many, that "God gave us two ears and one mouth. So he probably wants us to spend twice as much time listening as we do speaking."[1] You can resolve to change your habits of listening, and you can train yourself, successfully, to listen better.

---

1. *Christopher News Notes*, No. 234, undated.

The Most Difficult of All Learning Processes

It is a paradox that listening is both the easiest path to learning and the hardest study skill to master. Listening must be a self-taught skill, because it is the most difficult skill for a teacher to teach. Listening is least susceptible to discipline and is seldom accomplished, but the lack of this ability often makes the bore, so well defined by Ambrose Bierce, "A person who talks when you wish him to listen."

What then are the factors that make listening such a difficult skill to acquire? There are essentially four major ones: the listener must coordinate his mental processes with another person's, the speaker's; the listener must move through the topic at the same rate as this other person; the listener must follow the speaker's line of argument (even if he disagrees with the speaker's conclusions); and the listener must learn how to listen on his own.

The Problem of Coordination

Much of what you do in school is entirely within your control. Your reading, your thinking, your seeing—they are all subservient to your will, your abilities, and your desires. Listening is fundamentally different from these three other processes in that it involves another person, the speaker.

If you wish to think on a tangent as you read, you are free to do so, knowing that you can always take up where you left off reading. When listening, however, you must learn to put aside tangents, interesting though they appear, in order to coordinate your thinking with the thinking of the speaker. You must forfeit, briefly, your control over your thoughts in order to accept the ideas the speaker expounds. You are free later, after the lecture, to draw your own conclusions; but if you begin to do so during the lecture, you will not be following the speaker's ideas clearly, and so your listening will be less efficient.

The Problem of Speaking Rate

The second problem in learning to listen arises from lack of associated control. When you learn to read, your eyes control the speed with which you read. When you write, there is actual physical control in your hand. In thinking, the analysis of thought travels at exactly the speed capacity of your mind. But when you begin to train yourself to be a good listener, you are faced with a difficulty not unlike that of trying to drive a car without brakes. You can think four times as fast as the average teacher can speak. Only by demanding of yourself the most unswerving concentration and discipline can you hold your mind on the track of the speaker. This can be accomplished if the listener uses his free time to think around the topic—"listening between the lines," as it is sometimes called. It consists of anticipating the teacher's next point, summarizing what has been said, questioning in silence the accuracy and importance of what is being taught, putting the teacher's thoughts into one's own words, and trying to discern the test or examination questions that will be formed from this material. If you can train yourself to do this, you will save yourself much precious time by not having to read what has already been taught, and you will be able to give a more thoughtful and acceptable answer either in oral recitation or on a written test.

Learning to Follow the Leader

Perhaps you have not found it difficult to follow the captain of a team, the leader of your social group, or the mutually accepted director of your immediate circle of friends. This accepted leadership stems from common interest and mutual understanding. Learning to listen is learning to be a good follower, but in a totally different set of circumstances. First, there is the natural opposition between youth and age. You have great respect and love for your parents, teachers, and adult friends, but you cannot always agree that their ways of doing things and their approach to problems are the best ways for you. Your parents want you to listen in order that you may be saved from many of the experiences from which they were forced to learn "the hard way"; because they, like you, felt "misunderstood" and closed their minds when they were asked to become followers. Your teacher is talking about the problem on the blackboard, the passage in the textbook, the questions that are asked on examinations, because the experiences of others have demonstrated that help in these particular areas is essential to success.

The Problem of Working on Your Own

The fourth stumbling block in the way of those who would become good listeners is tradition. Until recently, within your own lifetime, listening was accepted as a state of mind rather than as a process of learning. Hours and years were spent teaching you to read, and you accepted it as basic to your future learning and success in school. Today, with the vast increase in the content demands of school subjects, plus the expanded use of audiovisual equipment, you now spend three times as much time listening as you do reading. Finding yourself in this situation is probably a bit puzzling. During all your years in school, you were often told to "Pay attention" or "Sit up and listen," but you were never actually trained how to be a good listener.

The distortions that arise from poor listening sometimes cause serious misunderstanding and make effective communication impossible. Sometimes they are amusing, but even these tend to show how little is heard or how easily it becomes something entirely different as it passes from one poor listener to another. One such distortion concerns the words shouted by John Wilkes Booth after he had shot Abraham Lincoln in Ford's Theater on the night of April 14, 1865. History has understood the words to be "Sic semper tyrannis," the state motto of Virginia. But a flagman on the Chicago, Aurora and Elgin Railroad gave Carl Sandburg another version. He had heard it differently: "This man Booth," said the flagman, "he shot the Prisident, jumped down onto the stage and hallooed, 'I'm sick, send fer McGinnis!'"

Few Do but Many Can

Columbia University Professor Jacques Barzun suggests that only the rarest minority ever accomplish the art of listening: "Now to learn to think while being taught presupposes the other difficult art of paying attention. Nothing is more rare: listening seems to be the hardest thing in the world. . . . In a lifetime one is lucky to meet six or seven people who know how to listen. . . . Lord Chesterfield was right when he wrote to his son that the power to listen is 'the mark of the civilized man.' The baby cannot listen; the savage and the boor will not. It is the boorishness of inattention that makes pleasant discussion turn into stupid repetitive argument, and that doubles the errors and mishaps of daily life."[2]

Psychologists and communications experts offer about the same picture. Through a series of extensive tests given after lectures, recordings, and discussions, they have compiled statistics that show that only a very small part of the population retain even 50 percent of what they have heard.

However, these communications experts point to a brighter future. Experimental courses taught to both young and adult groups have shown that listening is teachable, and can also be

2. Jacques Barzun, *Teacher in America* (Boston: Little, Brown and Co., 1945), 124.

self-taught. Many people have been able to double their listening proficiency in a matter of a few months. Encouraged by such reports, educators have added listening courses to school curriculums. One notable example is the one-year course being required of all freshmen at Michigan State University. The course first emphasizes that listening is an active process, not merely the reception of ideas. The workshop material consists of recorded outlines, speeches, simple word lists, and class lectures. Both students and teachers acclaim its success.

The Classroom as a Proving Ground

You can teach yourself to become a good listener. Each of your classrooms provides a practice laboratory. As you enter each, keep in mind the four basic difficulties you will have to overcome: (1) You must coordinate your listening and thinking powers with an outside force. (2) You must adjust to the difference in the speed of your thinking and the speed of the speaker. (3) You must be willing to follow. (4) You must accept the findings of research, and acknowledge listening as an essential and active learning process.

In addition to these four important steps to becoming a better listener, we offer a few suggestions for practice in the classroom and out. There are also several "don'ts" worth your consideration. Before you continue, however, it would be wise to answer the questions you may be asking: But what am I going to get out of all this practice? How much will I be able to raise my grades? Is it really possible to save time by listening in class?

Comparative studies of material given orally in class and material asked for on tests and examinations put the good listener in the driver's seat and ahead of the pack. In one history course, tape recordings revealed that 80 percent of the material asked for at testing time had been presented orally by the teacher. Some of the intelligent questions asked by students in the class were almost identical to the questions they saw later on tests. The percentage for science and mathematics classes was even higher. In several cases, demonstrations and associated material had presented the course so thoroughly that the good listener, capable of taking sufficiently detailed notes, could have achieved an honor grade without using either text or source book. Measurements of English classes proved difficult because of the points lost for mistakes in the mechanics of writing, but all comparisons of questions dealing with literature interpretation showed that the answers were given in class.

If you still question the chance to improve your grades by improving your ability to listen, try this simple experiment. As the class is being taught, write down what you think will be possible test questions. When testing time comes, see how many of your questions appear. If you give it a fair trial, you will need no further convincing.

Taking Notes: The Ultimate Key to Success*

Following naturally from good listening habits is skill in taking notes. Good note-taking requires action on your part: attentive listening, one-track thinking about what you hear, and active writing of key ideas.

The format of your notes is important. Put the date of the lecture and the name of the subject at the top of each page. Write the title of the lecture, if given, at the top of the first page. Divide your paper into two columns, using about one-third of the width for the left column. Write your notes only in the right-hand, wider column.

Emphasize important points by indenting, leaving spaces vertically, or underlining. These are quick methods of indicating importance.

* Also see Chapter 6 for more on note-taking.

Listen for key ideas, and write them down in your own words. Do not try to write down every word of the speaker; you will become a non-thinking "scribble-maniac" if you try to take such dictation. Notes in your own words will have more meaning when you review them later. Recall of material covered will be much easier, for putting notes in your own words has made them your personal knowledge.

Do not erase if you decide you have made an error. Simply draw a single line through the mistaken material. Such a practice is quicker than erasing and has the added benefit of leaving information on the page; you might find that it becomes useful later.

Do not copy your notes over to make them neat. Write them neatly in the first place. Rewriting notes is one of those useless wastes of time that hinders good studying.

As soon as possible, after the lecture, read your notes. As you read, fill in the gaps you may have left. Use the left hand column on the page to highlight information, writing there the important names, dates, technical information, or any other significant terms. Such reading is a kind of review that will serve to fix the lecture firmly in your mind, making study for tests and exams much easier. You should review your notes within twenty-four hours of taking them.

As you read your notes and highlight them, think actively about what you are reading. When you have finished, ask yourself questions about what you have read: what was this lecture about? what is the important information here? what might my teacher ask on the next test? It is helpful to write these questions at the end of your notes, for they will serve to organize any review you may do before tests and exams.

Note-taking, like learning to listen, requires practice. Even though you think all the material you need is in the textbook and associated reading, notes taken in class may make the reading easier by indicating those parts the teacher considers important.

Note-taking and listening complement one another. To become a good listener there is no better practice than note-taking. To lighten the burden of study outside of class and to improve your grade at the same time, there is nothing that rewards more than thoughtful, constant, informative note-taking in class.

Listening Aids

1. Estimate how much of the course material is taught in class, so you may see clearly the value of good listening.

2. Accept responsibility for gaining as much as you can by listening in class. The poor listener often has the attitude that the teacher has the responsibility somehow "to get the lesson" through to him. It is your responsibility to get through to the speaker and the lesson.

3. Listen for key words and clue phrases. Key words are those that carry great meaning and so serve as a kind of trigger for your memory. Clue phrases are the words that alert you to important information that follows; e.g., "this is important," "the three principle results are," or "you will be asked this on a test."

4. Always be ready, paper in place, pencil in hand, to take clear notes. If you rush frantically to get the materials ready after the speaker begins, you will miss most of the early parts of the lecture.

5. Ahead of time, prepare a work sheet to organize your thoughts and your note-taking. Such pre-planning will start you thinking about the topic even before the lecture begins. A work sheet that many have found successful is this:

WORKSHEET FOR NOTE-TAKING FROM LECTURES

I. Ask questions on topics from prior lecture, about which you need more information or explanation. Put the answers your teacher gives you in the appropriate place in your notes.

II. Preview

Write down in the space below what the lecture is going to be about, or what the title of the lecture is. (If you are not sure, ask your teacher.)

Take a minute to reflect on the title and predict what topics will be covered in the lecture.

III. Notes

Using the ⅓–⅔ format, write your notes. *Write key phrases and ideas only.*

Do not take dictation.

Leave the left-hand ⅓ of paper blank—to highlight important ideas or to fill in when teacher amplifies an idea.

Take notes in your own words in the right-hand ⅔ of the page.

IV. Question

Review your notes and:

1. Write questions to test your knowledge of what you have heard.

2. Write down questions about things you are not sure you understand, questions you need your teacher to answer at the beginning of the next class.

6. Make your listening three-dimensional: use your eyes, ears, and mind actively to pursue knowledge. Keep your eyes on the teachers and what they write on the blackboard. Keep your ears critically attuned so you may note what is important in the lecture and what is good or bad in the oral recitation of your fellow students. Keep your mind on the topic, thinking at the proper speed and building your capacity for judgment.

7. Use what you have learned from listening to prove your interest to the teacher and improve your grade. If the teacher has given more than the book offers, by all means, use it in your answers. Many a teacher, supposing that such was understood, has been asked, "May we use material from what we heard in class, or do you just want the answer from the book?" You can be sure that the part of the answer the teacher will value most is the part you got from listening.

Listening Errors to Avoid

Almost all the stupid, repetitive, and time wasting activity of the classroom, that robs people of the right to learn, arises from actions of people who, as described by Professor Barzun, are "afraid to lend their mind to another's thought, as if it would come back to them bruised and bent."[3] Here are a few listening "don'ts" for the classroom:

1. Don't interrupt in the middle of an explanation to say that you don't understand. If you wait until it's finished, you may have your question answered without having to ask it.

2. Don't be too fast with a related question. Until you have trained yourself to a degree of efficiency in listening, you will often be embarrassed by finding that your question has already been answered.

3. Don't display such impatience to speak, by frantically waving or tilting forward in your desk, as to indicate that the world's future depended upon what you had to say. Before you signal to speak, ask yourself, "Is this worth listening to?"—a far more important question than, "Is this worth saying?"

4. Don't clutter up the thought of those who wish to learn with insignificant and worthless contributions. That

3. Barzun, *Teacher in America* (Boston: Little, Brown, & Co., 1945), 232.

you saw *Macbeth* on television does not add to the class's knowledge of *Macbeth*. But if the scenery for Act II, Scene III, was unusual, both teacher and class might enjoy a brief description of it.

5. Don't hurry with that deadly phrase, "But I think" or "But I thought." If you have thought carefully, everyone will know from the quality of what you say.

6. Don't ever believe that speaking is more important than listening. It was Voltaire who said, "Men employ speech only to conceal their thoughts." And Socrates, one of the world's great philosophers, had the reputation of being the most patient and inquisitive listener in all Athens.

Daily Exercises in Listening

All the waking hours of the day provide myriad opportunities for practices to improve one's ability to listen. The requests made by parents that go unheard, the sounds of the world around you—the song of a bird, the interesting conversation of the two people seated next to you, the name of the person to whom you have just been introduced. The last is the one almost universal test of a poor listener. You are introduced to Tom McCabe or Joan Banks—simple sounds—yet five minutes later you say, "I'm sorry, but I missed your name." You heard the name with your ears only—your mind was making a critical assessment, your eyes were busy with the color of a jacket or dress, perhaps you were trying to place the person geographically. All these things could have followed the initial listening, but they replaced it instead. Here are some practices that will help you develop your ability to listen outside the classroom.

1. Make a resolution each morning for two weeks that during the day no one will have to repeat a single thing said to you.

2.   Practice selectivity. As you go to and from school, or wherever you go, or whatever you are doing, there are many sounds around you. Practice picking out those you wish to hear. Close your mind to all others. John Kieran, the naturalist, could sit amid cheering thousands at a football game in the heart of New York City and pick out the "honk, honk" of a Canada goose flying south high against the November sky.

3.   Start hearing the things you really enjoy. Do you really have to play the latest Bruce Springsteen record a dozen times to learn the words? The answer is "No." Test yourself—you can master the whole song with two playings.

4.   Form a team with a friend. Read each other poetry, sports scores, or whatever is of interest, and see what percentage the listener can repeat correctly.

5.   Recordings of speeches and literary readings are excellent for self-teaching. They are available at many public libraries.

6.   Develop a consciousness of your own speaking so that you will be clearly heard and understood. This will make a profound indirect contribution to your own listening ability.

Looking Back

1.   Here are three factors that hinder good listening:

    a.   You have to coordinate your mental processes with those of the speaker.
    b.   You must follow the speaker's line of argument.
    c.   You must teach yourself how to listen.

    What is the fourth factor?

2. One typical listening error we make is interrupting in the middle of an explanation to say we don't understand. Another is believing that speaking is more important than listening.

    What are two other "don'ts" that were listed in this chapter?

3. Can you fill in the blanks in these quotations that appeared in the chapter?

    a. (A bore is) "a person who _____ when you wish him to _____."
    b. "I'm sick, send _____ _____!"
    c. (The power to listen) "is the mark of the _____ man."
    d. "Men employ _____ only to conceal their thoughts."

THE CLASSROOM: ATMOSPHERE FOR ACHIEVEMENT

True Confessions

1. If you were the teacher and had to face a class of students like yourself, would you be pleased? Tell why.

2. If you were asked to contribute to an article entitled, "How to Drive Teachers Crazy," what would you write?

3. If you scrupulously followed all the school's rules and those of your individual teachers, would you be treated scornfully by your friends? If so, how would you handle the situation?

Important Elements of Classroom Success

While listening is an important part of classroom success, other elements contribute to creating an atmosphere for achievement in the classroom—or to making class time a wasteland of indifference and futility!

"If a man does only what is required of him he is a slave, the moment he does more he is a free man."[1] Be free—do more than the bare minimum, you will see the results.

Two important elements of classroom success are attitudes, yours toward your teachers and your work, and your teachers' toward you. Another is your style of work—good habits make for good work and for good attitudes, and go a long way toward creating the atmosphere for achievement. The contribution that you make toward maintaining an environment of learning will determine in no small degree what your mark will be. If you are to succeed, there must be an effective partnership between you and your teachers.

Partnership with the Teacher

Two simple tests can give you a sound estimate of how profitable this partnership is in your own case. First, make an estimate of what the class would be like if all the people in it acted and responded in the same way as you do. Would there be a general air of indifference and inattention, or would there prevail a sense of responsibility and willingness to learn? Would the class time be taken up with stupid questions and excuses for not being able to recite, or would intelligent discussion and well-organized recitation contribute much to all? It is important that this partnership be effective and produce the proper results. This partnership is in fact one of the greatest enterprises of your life. Your education, or lack of it, will make possible, or limit, opportunity and success for the remainder of your life.

Now examine the strength or weakness of this important joint venture by the second test—put yourself in the teacher's place. Is your work the quality that you would like if you were the teacher? Do you respond to correction and help as you yourself would like? If you were the teacher would you pick yourself as

---

1.   Marcus Tullius Cicero, a famous Roman.

one of the most diligent and cooperative members of the class? You may not be the smartest person in the class, but you can be the most responsive and appreciative.

Teachers know that they are not teaching to all the people in any given class. Some are there for the social ride, some because their parents require it, some because it's a state requirement, and some are there because they want to learn. If you were the teacher, in which of the groups would you place yourself? And if you were the teacher, one of the most complimentary things you could ever say about one of your students would be, "That youngster wants to learn." What do your teachers say of you?

The Influence of the Teacher

Other than your parents the person who will influence your life most will be a teacher. Literature has never wanted for apt description of the association between teacher and pupil, both humorous and serious. Here is a rather amusing but completely meaningful passage from a teacher in *The House Master* by Ian Hay:

> As a busily growing animal, I am scatter-brained and entirely lacking in mental application. Having no desire at present to expend my precious energies upon the pursuit of knowledge, I shall not make the slightest attempt to assist you in your attempts to impart it. If you can capture my unwilling attention and goad me by stern measures into the requisite activity, I shall dislike you intensely, but I shall respect you. If you fail, I shall regard you with the contempt you deserve, and probably do my best, in a jolly, high-spirited way, to make your life a hell upon earth. And what could be fairer than that?[2]

There is, of course, the other side of the coin, so definitively described by Gilbert Highet:

> Every teacher dislikes some pupils—the cheeky lipsticked adolescent girls, the sullen hangdog youths, the cocky vulgar little

2. Ian Hay, *The House Master* (Boston: Houghton Mifflin Co., 1928), introduction.

comedians, how loathsome they can be, all the more so because they do it deliberately! But if any teacher finds himself disliking all his pupils, he should change his character, and if that fails, change his job.[3]

"The teacher's influence," wrote Henry Adams, "reaches eternity, no one ever knows where it stops."

The Way to "Use" the Teacher

How you use your teachers is going to influence greatly your success in the classroom. Books of biography and autobiography are saturated with such influence that reached past the classroom into life. Thomas Jefferson wrote: "It was my good fortune, and what probably fixed the destinies of my life, that Dr. Wm. Small—a man profound in most of the branches of science, with a happy talent of communication, and an enlarged liberal mind—was my teacher." And Charles Darwin, writing of his life: "I have not yet mentioned a circumstance which influenced my whole career more than any other. This was my friendship with Professor Henslow—I became known as the boy who walks with Henslow."

Some of the things that you take for granted and seem insignificant and trivial are actually of greatest importance in making the classroom your arena of achievement. As the following hints imply, the way you behave in the classroom will affect the way you feel and think about your work, and also the way your teacher feels and thinks about you.

Hints on Attitude

1. Accept that learning is something no one can do for you. Learning is a lonely business, not a social affair. Even in the classroom, in the midst of your fellow stu-

3. Gilbert Highet, *The Art of Teaching* (New York: Alfred A. Knopf Co., 1950), 73.

dents, you will be learning on your own. If you expect the class to be a social affair, you will be disappointed.

Learning anything of value is difficult—hard, often tedious work; but remember, it has moments of joy and exhilaration arising from the warm inward feeling of achievement.

2.   Expect your teacher to require excellence. The teachers you remember as the ones who taught you the best are the ones who required honest work and never compromised the integrity of the class. They never disguised the true aim of the class behind a front of meaningless give-and-take or the absurdity of baseless argument.

3.   Know the implications of your questions before you ask them. What your questions imply will reveal much about your attitude. You want to show that you are sincere in your desire to learn and are not merely "going through the motions" of doing assignments. If you are assigned a composition, don't ask, "How long does it have to be?" Ask instead, "What do you wish us to include?" If you are not satisfied with a grade on written work, don't walk up to the teacher and protest, "Why'd you mark me off on this?" Ask instead, "How could I have improved this answer?" In each of these cases the former question carries negative implications, implications of hostility toward the teacher, while the latter question implies a sincere desire to improve. If you were a teacher, would you prefer a hostile, negative student, or a sincere one?

4.   Practice good classroom manners. Nothing can destroy the rapport of student and teacher so quickly, or permanently damage their essential partnership, as bad classroom manners and the absence of any effort toward improvement. Arrive in class on time and do not start looking at your watch halfway through the period. Do not start putting on your jacket and gathering up your books five minutes before the period ends. Important information is often given toward the end of class. Besides, what would a coach think of a player

who slacked off before the game was over? The way you carry your books, your posture as you sit at your desk or stand to recite, the manner in which you enter and leave the classroom—all these are either detrimental to or make a contribution to the "atmosphere for achievement."

Classroom efficiency is the product of self-respect, cooperation, and a willingness to learn. When you approach the teacher's desk to ask a question, stand erect, keep your hands by your side, and never lean over and put your hands on the desk. Coordinate your classroom manners to the methods of the teacher. If the teacher asks that questions be saved until the end of the period, do not interrupt in the middle. When you are late to class, be courteous enough to explain why at the end of the class. If you are absent from class, show enough concern to ask the teacher what you should get from someone who was present.

A little observation will reveal that the best students are those who maintain a high standard of classroom manners. They are aware that what is being done in the classroom is to help them learn. They are conscious of the continuing judgment that the interested and devoted teacher makes. Perhaps, save on isolated occasions, the student's only means of expressing gratitude and appreciation is through courtesy—from which all good classroom manners grow.

Accepting classroom instructions and following them puts you in the "atmosphere for achievement." Good habits are as easy to follow as bad ones, a good attitude as easy to develop as a bad one. The bad produce bad marks; the good, good marks. Nothing could be simpler than this. It becomes a matter of choice. Choose wisely.

What Kind of Student Are You?

How would you classify yourself as a participant in class? In light of the above hints, how would you rate your behavior as a student? Which of the following kinds of students are you?

1. Would you be an unprepared bluffer? This is the person who attempts to cover up his ignorance by asking unrelated questions or volunteering unreliable information gathered from comic books and movies.

2. Would you be the fluttering magpie? If you have attended the aviary at a zoo, you will probably remember that the one bird that could remain neither still nor quiet was the magpie. A student who is like the magpie interrupts constantly, always before he gives any thought to what he is going to say. More often than not, he repeats something that has been stated clearly and thoroughly already, and he repeats it inadequately.

3. Would you be the sensitive hopeful? This is the person who has prepared sufficiently to recite, but is afraid of what the teacher and other students will think of the recitation.

4. Would you be the accomplished leader? This is the student who has prepared the assignment, reviewed the essentials, and then established a point of view for possible oral discussion and a frame upon which to hang the answers to questions asked.

Developing Confidence in Your Abilities

There are many ways to become an accomplished leader. First try to make your attitude the best possible for the class. Then develop confidence in your abilities as a student. Here are some practical hints that will help you become well prepared and secure in your knowledge.

- Go to class with your assignments prepared. While this instruction may appear self-evident, it is all too common for students not to follow it, to prepare little or to prepare in such an inefficient manner as not to be able to use their knowledge to earn good grades. One way to check up on yourself is to ask yourself questions that will help to reveal the quality of your work.

To judge the quality of your written work, ask yourself these three questions. *First, am I pleased with what I have done?* It is futile to present work that identifies you as a sloppy, indifferent pupil. If your paper lacks form, neatness, and completeness, and you are content to turn it in—you are putting yourself on record as a person lacking in self-respect, willing to deal in mediocrity, whose sole aim is to get by. *Second, will my work satisfy the teacher?* Make sure that, even if you cannot complete the assignment, your work reflects sufficient responsibility and effort to portray your desire to do the very best of which you are capable. Follow carefully all the "mechanical" instructions: use appropriate paper, put the heading in the proper place, follow the specific instructions your teacher has given for the assignment. *Third, will my work be judged the best paper in the class?* Others may have more mastery of the subject, but no one can prevent you from making your best effort. Your teacher very quickly learns your capabilities and assesses the kind of effort you put forth. A good effort, even if you miss many answers, is a great booster of marks.

To judge the quality of your preparation for oral recitation, ask yourself these questions. *First, do I know enough to make a positive contribution to class discussion?* Since most teachers follow the textbook closely, you can, most of the time, predict what will be discussed in class. If you fear oral recitation, anticipate one or two topics you think likely for discussion and prepare for those topics. Knowledge will make you secure and help to overcome your fear. You also will learn that a sincere and honest recitation is not met by critical judgments. You probably will find, with a little inquiry, that you are not the only responsible student who fears reciting, but that only the bore and the clown operate brazenly.

Second, do I have an intelligent design for answering direct questions? Make the frame for your answer affirmative rather than negative. Do not start your answer by questioning the truth of your own statement. To begin with "Isn't it true?" or "Doesn't the book say?" casts doubt even before you have stated your point. Other "don'ts" include such introductions as "I don't know but," "I heard or read somewhere," "It seems to me," "I'm not sure, but I think." Design your answer to give your listeners assurance that you know what you are talking about. Try to make a quick blueprint before you start, particularly as to how you will end your answer. You will find it a painful experience if you shred a splendid answer by tacking on insignificant details merely because you have not anticipated a climax and a quick closing. Imagine your recitation as a one-minute drama that is to be properly staged; or imagine that for the period of your individual recitation you are the director of a meeting, controlling your audience and speaking so clearly that no one can help understanding.

Finally, how will my oral recitation be judged by the teacher and my fellow students? If you ask yourself the first two questions and can answer them honestly with a resounding YES, you will have answered this third question. Everyone will judge your answer favorably, all will judge you to be an accomplished leader!

- Go to class with the proper tools. Take your textbook. If you do not bring the text, you are revealing your lack of interest as flagrantly as if you wore a placard enscribed, "I HAVE NO INTEREST IN THIS CLASS." Take notebook, pen or pencil (well sharpened), pad for recording assignments, and special necessary tools such as compasses, protractors, calculators, and lab notebooks. If you were playing center field, and inning after inning went out without your glove, do you think your coach would keep you on the team for very long? Imagine going to a music lesson and forgetting to take your instrument or music. Arriving at a class without the tools will very quickly put you off the team or out of the lesson.

- Follow instructions. Write down, *clearly*, your assignments in a division of your notebook set aside for assignments or in a special assignment pad. Make sure you write down and follow the general instructions your teacher gives about the format for work done in the course. If your teacher asks, for example, for your name to be in the upper right-hand corner of the paper, put it there, every time.

Looking Back

1. You are doing a composition on the topic, "How to Win Friends and Influence Teachers." What are three commonsense suggestions you just read about that you might incorporate in your writing assignment?

2. As you examine the many hints for successful classroom behavior in Chapter 3, which one would you single out as being the most important? Explain the reasons for your choice.

3. In judging the quality of your preparation for oral recitation, you should ask whether you know enough to make a worthwhile contribution to class discussion and whether you know how to phrase direct questions properly.

    What was the third suggestion offered in the chapter?

4

STUDY TIME: DESIGN FOR SUCCESS

True Confessions

1. You have to turn in to your social studies teacher a long research paper on the causes of World War I. Is it likely that you will submit it on time? Why?

2. Have you ever budgeted your time in a written schedule? If not, why not? If so, tell why your plan did or did not work.

3. On December 22 your English teacher distributes a list of American novels, telling you to select one for reading during the upcoming vacation. Will you get the book on December 23, December 29, or January 3? Explain.

   One of your classmates who is certain to start on the book the night before the written report is due explains by saying, "I like to live dangerously." What other possible reasons are there for such bad habits?

Time Is Learning's Most Important Tool

The true value of study time can perhaps best be emphasized by an often quoted statement: "All genuine learning is self-education." The guidance and self-evaluation that the classroom offers are not to be discounted, but already admitting that "learning is a lonely business," it is not unreasonable to place premium value upon the time you spend alone in study. The great philosopher-emperor of Rome, Marcus Aurelius, said that "the present is the only thing of which a man can be deprived." And the Greek philosopher, Epicurus, pointed out that we ourselves are the deprivers: "But you, who are not master of tomorrow, postpone your happiness: life is wasted in procrastination." Procrastination is one of the most ruthless destroyers of time. In this chapter, specific and detailed methods for the proper use of this "our most limited blessing" will be considered.

Dr. William Osler, the renowned physician and teacher, used to say to beginning medical students, "How can you take the greatest possible advantage of your capacities with the least possible strain?" He answered the question in these words:

> By cultivating system. I say cultivating advisedly, since some of you will find the acquisition of systematic habits very hard. There are minds congenitally [born] systematic; others have a lifelong fight against an inherited tendency to diffuseness and carelessness in work. Take away with you, from a man who has had to fight a hard battle, the profound conviction of the value of system in your work. To follow the routine of the classes is easy enough, but to take routine into every part of your daily life is hard work. Let each hour of the day have its allotted duty, and cultivate that power of concentration which grows with its exercise, so that the attention neither flags nor wavers, but settles with a bull-dog tenacity on the subject before you. Constant repetition makes a good habit fit easily in your mind, and by the end of the session you may have gained that most precious of all knowledge—the power to work.[1]

Finding Where the Hours Go

Doubtless the first step toward establishing routine and order as regards the use of time is an awareness of where your weakness

1. Dr. Harvey Cushing, *The Life of Sir William Osler*, one volume edition (New York: Oxford University Press, 1940), 72.

lies and where you must begin the fight. It seems to be universally expressed, whether true or not, that there just isn't enough time. The person who leaves classes at 3:00 P.M. is sure there will be no difficulty in finding time to do the assignments before classes start at eight or nine the next morning. At least on the clock there is plenty of time—three hours (3:30–6:30) before dinner, three hours (7:00–10:00) after dinner. Six hours and four assignments, no need to rush, not more than an hour needed for each. "Certainly, I can walk with you to the drugstore. I can play tennis."

And after dinner the news was on television. Then there was a favorite program (just half an hour), or a new magazine had come in the mail. "Where did I leave my books? I think I'll check with a friend to be sure of the history assignment. Now it is 8:45 P.M. and I have to sharpen my pencil. I have sharpened my pencil. Which assignment should I do first? I have glanced at four books in quick succession. I have re-piled three of them. The fourth is open in front of me. I just brushed some dandruff off my sweater. I must look in the mirror to see whether or not my dandruff isn't getting worse."

It is now 9:10 P.M. The next morning, fifteen minutes before the first class, there is a last hopeless and futile attempt to cram into a few minutes what had once had hours for completion. Then is heard the oft-repeated lament—"there just isn't enough time."

This account of frittering away the hours is a pattern, with variations, that is enacted daily. Wishful thinking is a deep-seated human trait that carries us along, as with the current, the line of least resistance. It takes courage and action to face up boldly to how we use or abuse our time. So the first step toward the proper organization of time for better use is to find out what you are doing with your time at present.

Self-discovery and self-evaluation are the only really effective means of convincing yourself where your time goes. Make a time chart of your waking hours for one week, being completely honest with yourself, and record in as much detail as possible what you do. A simple chart to be conveniently kept in the front of your notebook might be made as follows:

TIME USE CHART
Monday, September 5

Hours	
A.M.	Arrived at School 8:30
8:00–9:00	Talked with friends 8:30–9:00
9:00–10:00	Chemistry Class
10:00–11:00	Study period.
	Went to school library—read magazine.
11:00–12:00	History class
P.M.	Lunch for half hour.
12:00–1:00	Cannot remember what I did until 1:00 P.M.
1:00–2:00	English Class
2:00–3:00	Math Class
3:00–4:00	3:00–3:30 travel home
	3:30–4:00 snack, telephone, etc.
4:00–5:00	Met friend at drugstore
5:00–6:00	Read English assignment 15 min.
	Listened to records.
6:00–7:00	Dinner
7:00–8:00	
8:00–9:00	
9:00–10:00	

TOTALS—12 hours (excepting 2 for meals)

Time in class	4
Time studying outside of class	_____
Time in social activity and recreation (talking, drugstore, telephone, records, etc.)	_____
Time otherwise accounted for	_____
Time not accounted for	_____

Do the same for each day of the week. At the end of the week, make a total for the entire week. Do not be embarrassed by your findings. Be convinced that you can rearrange and re-allot your time to greater advantage. If one week's trial does not convince you, carry the experiment through a second or third week.

Psychologists and efficiency experts have done much research in the advantage of organized time. The results of this research are very convincing. They show the tremendous value in time saving. They show the effectiveness of work approached with a definite job in mind rather than the question "What next?" as is the approach of many students to their studies. Research has shown that the energy saved through good organization is directed toward the job at hand. Consequently, one of the significant benefits of organization, system, and a well–worked-out schedule for study, is the power that organization makes available.

Busy, but Well Organized

It is interesting to note from the same surveys that students who have part-time jobs, afternoons or week-ends, manage to find more study time than those who have nothing in the nature of definite time responsibility. The student who is paid for two hours of his labor has learned that time has value—dollars and cents value. At the place of afternoon employment, he is required to start at 3:30. He can't decide to do something else until 4:00; thus he receives basic training in doing things by schedule. Having less time for study probably forces him to budget his time more accurately than those with more time. Whatever the reasons, the results are the same. In almost every case the person with less time available found more time for study and made better grades.

The title of this chapter, "Study Time: Design for Success," contains the magic word—*Design*. How then shall you design your time in order to avoid all the problems noted above, use your capacities to better advantage with less strain, and at the same time boost your grades? There are two possible designs.

The first you can buy ready-made in the form of a plan book. It might have the title, "Teacher's Plan Book," but do not let this disturb you. One such is the Milton Bradley Plan Book, available from The Milton Bradley Co., Springfield, Massachusetts. Your teacher would probably be able to recommend others equally as good. The days of the week will be divided into periods sufficient in number to take care of your classes and study periods, with space left over for afternoon and evening planning. In appearance a week's schedule would be approximately as the model that follows, except about six times larger, each space being sufficient to write in assignments or what to study. Classes and study periods are filled in to indicate how your schedule might look when completed. Along with each class the assignment could be included. That is one reason why a plan book with thirty weeks, covering the entire school year, is advantageous.

TIME SCHEDULE

Subject Period Time	Monday	Tuesday	Wednes- day	Thursday	Friday	Saturday
Math. I 9:00– 10:00	*Math Pages 1–5 Exercise 2 Problems 1–8*	*Math*	*Math*	*Math*	*Math*	
English II 10:00– 11:00	*English Julius Caesar Act I Pages 1– 34*	*English*	*English*	*English*	*English*	*Study History for Mon.*
Study III 11:00– 12:00	*Study Math for Tues.*	*Study Math for Wed.*	*Study Math for Thurs.*	*Study Math for Fri.*	*Study Math for Mon.*	*Study English for Mon.*
French IV 1:00–2:00	*French Review Exer. Vocab. p. 10*	*French*	*French*	*French*	*French*	

TIME SCHEDULE (*continued*)

Subject Period Time	Monday	Tuesday	Wednes-day	Thursday	Friday	Saturday
History V 2:00–3:00	*History* Problems in Democracy Pages 5–17	*History*	*History*	*History*	*History*	
End of School 3:00–3:30 3:30–4:00	Band Prac. Going Home	Band Prac.	Band Prac.	Band Prac.	Band Prac.	
4:00–5:00	Exercise Recreation	Same	Same	Same	Same	
5:00–6:00	Study French for Tues.	Study French for Wed.	Study French for Thurs.	Study French for Fri.	Study French for Mon.	
7:00–8:00	Study History for Tues.	Study History for Wed.	Study History for Thurs.	Study History for Fri.		
8:00–9:00	Study English for Tues.	Study English for Wed.	Study English for Thurs.	Study English for Fri.		
9:00–10:00	Read, Review, Rest	Same	Same	Same		

The approximate size of each period would be as follows:

Monday

> *Math*
> Pages 1–5
> Exercise 2
> Problems 1–8

There is sufficient space for recording the assignment skeleton. Details would have to be written into your regular notebook.

TIME SCHEDULE

Twelve Precious Hours	Monday	Tuesday	Wednes-day	Thursday	Friday	Saturday	Sunday
8:00–9:00	8:00–8:30 Bus to school Review one subject						
9:00–10:00	Chemistry Class						
10:00–11:00	English Class						
11:00–12:00	Study Chem. for Tues.	Study Chem. for Wed.	Study Chem. for Thurs.	Study for Chem. test on Fri.	Study Chem. for Mon.	Study English for Mon.	
1:00–2:00	Math Class					Good study time	
2:00–3:00	History Class						
3:00–4:00	Home and Exercise						
4:00–5:00	Recreation			Study for Chemistry Test			
5:00–6:00	Study Math for Tues.	Study Math for Wed.	Study Math for Thurs.	Study Math for Fri.	Study Math for Mon.		
7:00–8:00	Study Hist. for Tues.	Study Hist. for Wed.	Study Hist. for Thurs.	Study Hist. for Fri.	Study Hist. for Mon.		
8:00–9:00	Study Eng. for Tues.	Study Eng. for Wed.	Study Eng. for Thurs.	Study Eng. for Fri.	Recreation		
9:00–10:00	Relax and Read	Listen to Music					
	Comments All work finished	Comments	Comments	Comments	Comments A good week Grades up	Comments	Comments

Some students prefer a second design for their work schedule, one without space for assignments. Of course, one copy of such a schedule in front of your notebook and another copy posted where you study would suffice, perhaps with minor changes, for the entire school year. Such a schedule is usually divided into twelve working hours between 8:00 A.M. and 10:00 P.M., leaving an hour free for lunch and one for dinner. Such a schedule might resemble the model on page 38.

There is much to commend each type of schedule, but many students prefer the latter. Only one day, Monday, is filled in fully. Several things are very important if a schedule is to work effectively. Notice that the period from 11:00–12:00 is used to study the same subject each day. The same is true for 5:00–6:00, 7:00–8:00, and 8:00–9:00. Research has shown that doing the same thing at the same time each day makes the work seem much easier because it does away with the energy-consuming self-conflict and the confusion of deciding "What next?" It becomes a part of you—not a force outside with which you have to contend.

The schedule also shows you there is much time that can be used for the things you want to do—perhaps more, actually, than you have ever thought available. Saturday and Sunday have been left almost blank, but it is very wise to make a sensible apportionment of time for study and reading. If you have a part-time job, you will probably find it easy to allot this time. Two interesting results have been noted from the study of proper time usage. First, the more one has to do the easier it is to make a workable schedule and follow it. Second, people who plan carefully study fewer hours and get better grades than people who do not restrict themselves to allotted time, but kid themselves into believing that they study all the time. The person who works without a schedule is the one who fails a test and then complains, "But I studied three-and-a-half hours." What this person admits is that three-and-a-half hours were spent seated with a book, daydreaming, thinking fuzzy thoughts at the edge of the subject but never really getting into it.

People who follow a schedule of work train themselves to concentrate. Problems in concentration are, in fact, problems in the effective use of time. The person who sets a limit of time to complete a job makes a choice between getting the job done or dreaming in a half-hearted way for an equally indefinite period of time.

The first of all good study habits is the proper use of time. A well-organized schedule, followed until it becomes a natural part of living, brings into existence the second great aid to study— the ability to concentrate. From the combined results of these two comes the power of work; and from the power of work, not from wishful thinking or idle dreams, come the better grades for which you strive.

It is within your power to bring productive and effective order into your life. The suggestions that follow can make a time schedule work for you; and take half the confusion, worry, indecision, and effort out of your study.

Making Your Schedule Work

1. Give your schedule a fair chance. After you have evaluated your loss of time without a schedule and have prepared a working schedule, do not expect procrastination, resistance, and self-deception to disappear at once. A month of diligence and discipline is perhaps the minimum time necessary for developing the habit of going from one activity to study, or from class to study, or from study of one subject to another, without loss of time or the power of concentration.

2. Put your schedule to work in a definite place. Place is as important as time in making your schedule work. If you study in a study hall or the library at school, always sit at the same desk or table. Have what you need— pencils, paper, books—when you sit down, and discipline yourself not to move until a certain block of work has been finished. If you study at home, it should be in a quiet place, well-lighted, and facing away from the window. Put all distractions out of reach and sight if possible. Your friend's picture, magazines, unan-

swered letters, will pull you away and waste your time because you will lose your power of concentration.

If it is noisy at home, study in the public library. The library offers the best of all atmospheres for study; the setting, the quiet, the presence of books and other people deep in concentration will all aid in helping you put your schedule into effect.

Do not kid yourself by thinking that you can study and listen to music, catch snatches of television, or listen to people talk. It cannot be done, and this has been proved by numerous tests and experiments. There is no common ground where study, relaxation, and sociability meet. There is a place for study and a place for relaxation and sociability. If you attempt to make them the same, your study schedule will never work.

3. Study the same thing at the same time each day. This further strengthens the good habit of action by second nature. It also eliminates the exception—always troublesome and causing some delay. You are prepared mentally for the thing you are used to doing with regularity. Mental preparation is the first step toward concentration.

4. Fit your schedule to your needs. You know your capacities. One subject will take you longer than another. Learn to measure your concentration span. If you can only work effectively for half an hour, fit your schedule with a five-minute period to take your eyes and mind off the work before you.

5. Do not be too heroic in making your first schedule. If you make yourself into a relentless "grind" for two weeks, you might find a schedule so thoroughly distasteful as to never endure long enough to appreciate its true purpose—which is to make your work easier and to provide you with freedom, not sentence you to constant drudgery.

6. Do not be afraid to change your schedule to take care of emergencies and ever-recurring natural variations that arise.

A very important part of your education is to learn to be able to judge between conflicting interests. When changes occur, try to keep the pattern of the day and week as nearly regular as possible. All changes must be followed through to their final conclusions. For example, on the model schedule, if you decide to play basketball Thursday afternoon between four and five, you must decide on time to study for the chemistry test. Not to do so is to find yourself in trouble and also defeat the purpose of the schedule.

A time schedule is a design for success, not only in school but in life. The work habits of the people in the world who have achieved success and accomplished the happy life invariably show a well-designed work pattern. These are the people who make their schedule of accomplishment one of the chief responsibilities of their lives. If you aim at success in school and in life, you can do no less.

Looking Back

1. What are the only really effective means of convincing yourself where your time is spent?

2. It seems a paradox that students who have less time for study often manage to do more studying than the rest of the class. How can you explain it?

3. How would you answer the classmate who said, "I don't make schedules because I know I won't be able to live up to them"?

5

MASTERING ASSIGNMENTS: METHODS OF STUDY

True Confessions

When asked how they study for a biology test, several sophomores replied:

1. "I flip the book's pages quickly, stopping only on those sections that look unfamiliar, and I reread them carefully. I don't waste time on what I already know."

2. "I look over my answers to the homework questions, review the quizzes we had during the marking period, and spend an hour discussing possible test questions with the brightest kid in the class."

3. If the test covers two or three units in our biology book, I will read them over, scan the questions at the end of the chapters, and then check over my class and lab notes."

4. "I pray earnestly!"

What is your evaluation of the various answers?

Difference Between Reading and Studying

After you have worked to create the climate for study, to allot time and to keep your assignments straight, you must get down to the serious business of studying. Too often people equate serious study with long hours of reading and rereading. Several years ago a psychologist was asked to help Maxwell Air Force Base officers improve their efficiency in studying. As he began his work, he discovered a remarkable thing: "When a number of them [who requested] help were asked if they had forgotten how to study, almost every one replied, 'No—I never learned.'"[1] They had found out, the hard way, the difference between reading and study.

When doing school work, you will improve your efficiency greatly by using proper methods of study. Remember that studying includes more than reading, it includes classification and recall of information. In order to understand what a good study method is, it is helpful to reflect on how the mind works.

Study Methods

There are many study methods, each of varying complexity. They all have the basic aim of enhancing your ability to sort out meaningful information from what you read and to recall it accurately.

- A good study method will contain a part devoted to previewing. Previewing is an apt term, for as the student "*pre*-views" his assignment, he is looking ahead, looking for the highlights of the assignment. In so doing, the student begins the process of perceiving the orderliness of the information contained in the assignment. To preview effectively, you should read the introductory par-

1. Thomas F. Staton, *How to Study*, 4th ed. (Nashville: McQuiddy Printing Co., 1954), preface.

agraph, the bold face type, and the summary paragraph at the end of the assignment. If the assignment contains none of these, you may preview by reading the topic sentences of each paragraph. The topic sentences are usually the first or second sentence of the paragraph and will tell you what the paragraph is about. If the lesson contains review or study questions at the end of the chapter, you should include reading them as part of the preview. By reading quickly in this way, you will be able to gain an overview of the assignment.

Imagine yourself on a journey; first, you consult a map to find the best way to reach your destination. When you have found your map and route you begin to think of preparing for the journey, making sure you have what is necessary to complete the trip. For a journey by car, you will need gas, toll money, and the knowledge of route numbers; on a journey through your assignment, you will need paper and pencil (gas and toll money), the knowledge of the path the line of argument will take, what the information you will be reading is (the route numbers). A good preview, like a good map, will help you to begin to sort out information as you read. It will substantially increase your ability to put the information you read into meaningful groups and will increase your ability to remember what you have read.

Statistics should not be necessary to offer certification for what so plainly is a good commonsense practice, but knowing the skepticism with which youth hears adult advice, test results might be convincing. Two hundred students, representing various high school subjects, were separated into two equal groups. One group was taught to use the preliminary survery as the first step in studying an assignment. Each group was clocked for the length of time used for study, and each group was given identical tests on the material studied. The group using the preliminary survey was found to study 30 percent less time and average seven points higher when tested. Individual tests from among the same groups showed that some individuals had more comprehension of the material using only a preliminary survey than some students who read the whole assignment without a survey. The students using the survey spent about ten minutes for previewing while the others used about forty minutes to read the whole assignment.

- The second part of a good study method is reading the assignment. You should read carefully but quickly, reading for ideas. As you read for ideas, you should write them down in your notebook in your own words or underline the key phrases in your textbook, if you are fortunate enough to own your personal copy. You will find, if you have done the preliminary survey, that reading will go fairly quickly, more quickly than you are accustomed to reading. The reason for your increased speed is that the preview has started you thinking about the topic you are studying and has put the major areas of discussion in your mind, thus enhancing your ability to sort out the information and make sense of it. In order to read the assignment quickly and thoroughly, you must be alert and take an active part in the process. If you remain passive, letting the words wash over you, you will not be able to find the main ideas quickly, and you will have to reread the assignment, losing the time you saved by having done the preview!

- The third part of a good study method is review. After you have read the assignment, you should reflect upon what you have read. Reflecting is not rereading; it is, instead, the active use of your mind to recall what you have read, what the major ideas were in the assignment. As part of the review, you should ask yourself questions to test your knowledge of the assignment. You will find if you ask yourself questions, that you will be anticipating the questions your teacher will be using during the following class period or on tests.

Experiments with a group of high school freshmen at Kent School, during which the students kept their questions in writing, showed that after six weeks of practice, they anticipated and prepared for 80 percent of the questions asked by their teacher in class. Experiments with juniors at the same school, and among juniors in several public high schools, showed that students trained in a study method that omitted any questioning process averaged nine points less on identical tests than students who used a study method that incorporated questions.

A good study method, then, employs three major parts: *a preliminary survey, a careful but quick reading for key ideas,* and *a review.* The following are some study methods that others have developed and found useful. Look them over to see whether they appeal to you. Notice that while they all contain more than the three basic parts, each of them has parts that conform to our discussion above.

In 1946 Dr. Francis P. Robinson brought forth a volume entitled *Effective Study,* in which he explained a study method that he had devised. He called this method the SQ3R method since it contained five steps: Survey, Question, Read, Review, Recite.[2]

The following is an explanation of each of the five steps.

SQ3R

SURVEY Reading bold face type, topic sentences, summary paragraphs, review questions, will give you an idea of the contents of the assignment.

QUESTION After you have completed the survey, ask yourself what will be the important information contained in the assignment. Questioning will also help you to link the information in the assignment to what you already know. An easy way to create the questions is to turn the bold face type or the topic sentences into questions.

READ Read for ideas; especially, to answer the questions you have created. Read one section at a time, and then go to the next step.

RECITE Answer the questions you have asked, without looking at your notes or at the textbook. After

2. Dr. Francis P. Robinson, *Effective Study* (New York: Harper & Bros., 1946), 13.

you have finished answering the questions, go on to the next section of the assignment, read it, and answer the questions you have asked. Continue reading and reciting until you have finished the assignment.

REVIEW   After you have finished the assignment, look away from the book, go over your notes, and get a comprehensive grasp of the complete assignment.

Dr. Thomas F. Staton, as mentioned earlier, worked to help Air Force officers improve their study habits. He devised a study method that is slightly different from Dr. Robinson's. Dr. Staton called his method the PQRST method since he named its five parts: Preview, Question, Read, State, Test.[3]

Below is an explanation of the parts of Dr. Staton's method. Notice the similarities to and differences from Dr. Robinson's method.

PQRST

PREVIEW   Read the topic headings, the summary paragraphs, the review questions, or if these are not present, the topic sentences of the paragraphs. Try to associate this assignment to previous work in class or to previous assignments.

QUESTION   Ask yourself what is important in the assignment. Try to turn the topic headings into questions.

READ   Read the assignment carefully but quickly, looking for key ideas. Take notes or underline in the textbook (if you are fortunate enough to own you personal copy). Be judicious both in note-taking and in underlining. Non-specific note-taking is time consuming and ultimately useless because it does not organize your notes or your thinking. Too much underlining also is non-specific and does not organize your thinking; you will lose the key ideas in the mass of underlining.

3. Staton, *How to Study*, 1–12.

STATE   Answer the questions you created at the beginning. State what was important that you neglected to ask questions about.

TEST   Review your knowledge of the assignment. Ask
yourself questions, and answer them. Be as detailed as is necessary, but do not bog yourself
down with so much detail that you lose the key
ideas.

We also have devised a study method, one we call Four Steps
to Mastery. Below is an explanation of its parts. As before, notice the similarities to and differences from the other methods.

4S = M
(Four Steps Equal MASTERY)

PRELIMINARY SURVEY   Recall yesterday's assignment, and associate it to the
new assignment. Read topic
headings, summary para-
graphs, study questions, or if
the textbook lacks these, the
topic sentences of the paragraphs.[2]

READING THE   Read for ideas, do not read
ASSIGNMENT   word by word. Turn the units
of thought of the chapter into
questions.

QUICK REVIEW   Retrace your steps quickly
through the assignment by
skimming, looking for the
main ideas.

SUMMARIZE THE   Write, if you can, a summary
ASSIGNMENT   that contains all the important information found in the
assignment. If you lack the
time to write the summary,
prepare it mentally.

The best study methods will cause you to think carefully about
your assignments and put information into new categories. They

will enable you to make the relationships between information stand out and make your own sense of what you read. In making your own sense out of the assignment, you have made the assignment part of you and thus much easier to remember. The study methods also have the benefit of organizing vast quantities of information into manageable groups, so that when you review for tests and exams, you will be studying from well-organized notes and will not be forced to create order out of chaos in the limited amount of time available at term exam time.

Making Good Study Methods Work

1. Expect new study methods to produce results. You must be convinced that better habits will (a) help you find what you are expected to learn, (b) understand it more rapidly, (c) fix it in your mind more easily, and (d) improve your recitation and grades. Once convinced, discipline yourself against the hazards to learning. One that is typical, and causes many muddled and incorrect answers is that of trying to cram at the beginning of class, sometimes even while the teacher is making an announcement or assignment. Such an act betrays either lack of preparation or lack of confidence. The impression made by such practice upon the teacher is one of indifference to good habits of study and poor planning.

2. Use whatever tactics are necessary to keep all study periods active. Inaction is true learning's worst enemy. The long, gruelling marathon is not study—avoid it. Several short periods, during which a keen sense of proper methods is kept in the front of the mind, are much better than a period that is lengthened into boredom. Experiments show that 25 percent higher grades are made on material studied a half hour each day for five days than one session of two and one half hours. Remember this practice for preassigned tests and examinations.

3. All good study habits require an alertness for the effective use of textbook clues and built-in aids. Learn to watch for clues that lead into the "larger meaning" as opposed to those that introduce enumerated material. Use introductory paragraphs, summary paragraphs, topic and summary sentences. Pay close attention to boldface and italics, and all numbered items. Writers of manuals during World War II found that soldiers could learn material more easily if it was arranged in short paragraphs and numbered one, two, three, etc. Textbooks are not written to be read as one reads a novel. They are organized to present a specific amount of material in a definite way. An alterness as to how the material is presented aids in the discovery of study clues. Special attention should be paid to illustrations, diagrams, maps, and charts. Much of the most significant material of the text is often given this graphic treatment.

4. Do not let details ruin your vision and perspective. Even though small portions of material are handled in study, avoid getting lost in detail. The first question, and one whose importance cannot be overlooked, is, "What am I supposed to learn from this assignment?" Failure to recognize *the larger meaning and patterns of relationship* leads to a condition not unlike trying to hold a dozen eggs in each hand without a basket. Package your details so that you can manage them.

5. Use your common sense to judge which study methods are best for you. Only you can evaluate whether or not your preparation is easier and your recitation more thorough by use of questions before or after reading. Only you can judge whether you need to write "working notes" for your review or whether you can handle it orally. Practice with different methods is the only honest means of arriving at a sound judgment, and only you can accomplish the conscientious practice.

6. Do not assume that good study methods are indeed quite simple and not markedly different from your old

reading and guessing method. Directions for bowling, playing tennis, swimming, driving an automobile, playing a guitar, all sound quite simple when you are reading them. But learning any new skill requires much in adaptation and practice. If you learn to use effective study methods, you will have adopted new habits for old, and practiced equally as seriously as at your other accomplished skills. The skill of study, if you are willing to devote the time to it, will prove far more important than all your other skills combined, for directly and indirectly, it will make a contribution to all.

7.   Prepare a work sheet for each assignment.

4S = M Worksheet for Reading Assignments

Step 1   *Preliminary Survey*

    a.   What do I know already about this assignment from what I have learned in class?

    b.   Find out what topics the assignment covers by reading the summary at the end of the chapter and make a list of the topics.

    c.   If there is no summary paragraph, but there are study questions, read the study questions to find out what topics the assignment covers. Write a list of the topics.

Step 2   *Reading the Assignment*

    a.   Read the assignment *actively,* looking for the topics you have listed in part b or c of step one above. Turn major thought units of the chapter into questions.

    b.   Write the page number(s) on which you find the topics you have listed or on which you find the answers to the study questions.

    c.   Take notes in outline form, using the ⅓–⅔ format on your page.

    d.   If you draw a map of the chapter, make sure to allow space for revising and highlighting your map.

Step 3 *Quick Review*

    a. Answer orally the study questions found at the end of the chapter.

    b. Orally, recite the topics covered in the assignment (if there are no study questions).

    c. Write down the topics covered in the assignment that you were unable to predict during your Preliminary Survey.

    d. Write down questions you think your teacher might ask on a test.

Step 4 *Summarizing the Assignment*

    a. Write a summary of all the important information found in the assignment.

    b. If you lack the time to write the summary, prepare it mentally.

Prepare worksheets for your assignments using this model as your guide. If you leave enough space between the lines of directions on the worksheet, you can put both your list of topics covered and your summary of the assignment right on the worksheet. After you have taken your notes on the assignment, place your study sheet in your notebook directly in front of the pages containing your notes. By doing this you will give yourself a kind of introduction to your notes, a covering sheet which is standardized and which briefly will tell you what is covered in more detail in your notes. You will find it helpful when you are studying for major tests or term examinations to have these worksheets already prepared for they will help you study more efficiently and quickly.

Looking Back

1. The SQ3R method involves Survey, Question, Read, Recite, and Review. The 4S = M system stands for Four Steps = Mastery. What does PQRST stand for?

Tell why you would (would not) use one of these techniques in the future.

2. a. The first basic part of a good study method is to preview the assignment. What are the two other parts?

   b. Assume that you had to explain the preview technique to a beginner. In fifty words or fewer, what are the salient points you would tell him about previewing?

3. All schools have many different courses of study, and some even have administrators in charge of curriculum development. It is rare, however, for a school to offer a course in "How to Study." How do you explain that oversight?

   Write a letter to you local superintendent of schools to get his opinion on the feasibility of giving such instruction.

6

NOTE-TAKING: SUMMARIES, OUTLINES, MAPS

True Confessions

1. If you had to rely solely on the material in your notebook, would it help you to review for your tests? What is the strongest point of your note-taking? The weakest?

2. Sir Francis Bacon wrote, "To spend too much time in studies is sloth." Before you throw your cap up in the air and rejoice about that statement, explain what you think he meant. Can you see a more sophisticated meaning?

3. Samuel Johnson, the great eighteenth century man of letters, called note-taking a "necessary evil." Tell why you agree or disagree with Johnson.

Kinds of Notes

After you have chosen a good method of study, you will need to learn how to take good notes, so that you will have a clear record of what you have learned. You will need these notes to reduce the quantity of words you read while studying and to make important information easy to remember.

There are three basic kinds of note-taking: writing summaries, writing outlines, and drawing maps. Each of these fulfills both of the functions of note-taking, but each form is unique. All three assist the learner in graphically picturing the basic structure and meaning of what he is studying while aiming at compactness and clarity.

Format

Whatever style of note-taking you use, format is extremely important. Consistency is also important. If you use the same system of indicating importance, such as indenting, spacing, or underlining on each page of your notes, your mind will perceive the key information with a minimum of effort.

You should, when writing summaries and outlines, always divide your paper into two columns, using about one-third of the width of the page for the left-hand column. Write your notes only in the right-hand column. Use the left column to highlight your notes by writing key names, terms, dates, or ideas. Write your highlights when you review your notes.

The left column also gives you space for adding to your notes at a later time. If your teacher gives more information about a topic that you have already put in your notes, you may write the new information in this left-hand column, thus enhancing your notes, while not disorganizing them.

The Making of a Good Summary

A summary gives in condensed form the main points of a body of material. To create a good summary, you must abide by the following rules. (1) Omit no fundamental idea. (2) Introduce no new ideas. (3) Leave out all editorial or general statements. (4)

Maintain the point of view of the text. (5) Write in your own words.

As you are writing your summaries, beware of one common fault in writing condensations. All too often students write down sentences taken from the text, without relating them to one another. Such a grouping of unrelated sentences is not a summary, it is merely a chopped up version of the original. On the other hand, a condensation—whether it be a summary, précis, or synopsis—is a small composition, beginning with a topic sentence, with major ideas and minor ideas all clearly identified, and with smooth transitions between parts.

If you write a summary, précis, or synopsis, you will gain several advantages: (1) a clear set of notes for review, (2) an improved ability to think and condense, (3) practice in recognizing the main points in what you read (what is important), (4) a good memory aid (your own words are easier to remember than someone else's), and (5) practice in organizing and writing smooth and complete short compositions.

Summary writing starts as a challenge. Reducing sentences to phrases, phrases to meaningful words, will require practice and the study of summaries written by others. Examine the essays in reference books; they really are summaries and are the best examples you can find to emulate. Economy of words can become an important part of your learning, a time saver, and also help improve your marks. The length of a summary will vary according to your purpose and the requirements of your teachers. However, for your own review summaries, try to keep them below one-third of the size of the original text. If after extensive practice you can reduce them to one-fifth, it is all the better. A well-written summary is a test of how completely you have understood a paragraph, a chapter, an assignment, or a book; and of how concisely and clearly you have been able to shorten it without loss of meaning.

Examine the sample summary that follows. It is a summary of Chapter 2, on listening. Note the format, especially the highlighting in the left column.

LISTENING: THE EASY WAY TO LEARN

4 stumbling blocks to good listening

There are four stumbling blocks to good listening. The listener must: (1) coordinate his thoughts with the speaker's, (2) slow down his rate of thinking to match the rate of speaking, (3) follow the line of argument of the speaker (even if he disagrees), and (4) overcome the lack of emphasis on listening as a skill to be learned. Few people truly listen well, many hear only part of what is being said. Those who practice listening in class benefit because much of the material of a course will be given orally, perhaps as much as 80 percent. People who listen well also take good notes: writing in their own words, writing neatly, and writing down only key ideas. Those who practice listening well: listen for key words, have note-paper and pencil ready, prepare a work sheet, listen three dimensionally (ears, eyes, mind). Also, those who practice listening well avoid: interrupting the speaker, asking questions quickly, impatience, making worthless comments, and expressing their opinions.

up to 80 percent of course material given orally

listening aids

listening errors

Finding Models of Condensing

If you have difficulty summarizing, even after honest attempts at practice, you will find it helpful to examine some models of condensing.

Look in a junior encyclopedia, such as *World Book* or *Junior Britanica*. Read the summarization of the history of your state or city. Read several biographies. Note carefully the division of topics, the choice of words, and the use of graphic material in dealing with population, industry, and resources. If there are one-volume encyclopedias on the reference shelf, compare the facts of an article in one of them with an article about the same topic found in a ten-volume work.

Equally as valuable as seeing how material is summarized is to learn what summaries exist ready at hand to help you. Are you enjoying your algebra class? Is the study of chemistry proving difficult for you? Are you confused about "Jacksonian Democracy" as it is presented in your textbook? Look up *algebra* in the encyclopedia. Here you will find the course, its principle parts, the methods of solving equations, and illustrations to clarify difficult problems. From a four-page summary your whole conception of the course may be changed. You may really understand for the first time what algebra is all about. Do the same for your chemistry. The enlightenment resulting from such a brief inquiry can change both your attitude, your understanding, and your mark. Check "Jacksonian Democracy" in a junior encyclopedia, then in a larger one, or in an encyclopedia of history. It is so easy to learn if you bother to give a little thought to finding what you want.

Perhaps you have more than once been in a situation similar to the student who reading Homer's *Iliad* in poetry translation, could not follow the thread of the story. After much persuasion, he looked up the *Iliad* in the encyclopedia. There he found it summarized by books. Book II, which was causing the reader so much trouble, was summarized in nine lines; and the whole twenty-four books, the thread of the story plainly given, in three-and-a-half pages. From this time on, the student did not have to be persuaded to use the summaries available to him. He was able to read the *Iliad* and enjoy it. He discovered that the reference shelf in the library was filled with study aids, waiting to be used to clarify and save time.

Books of facts, general encyclopedias, encyclopedias of specific subjects—history, literature, science—all contain summarized material that can provide quick clarification. Atlases, handbooks, dictionaries of all kinds, beckon from the reference shelf in the library. The use of carbon-14 to explain that Cro-Magnon man's campfire in a cave in France burned 11,000 years ago sounds complicated and difficult. Look it up in a reference book. The whole process is summarized in half a column.

Weekly news magazines and book reviews often provide excellent examples of good summarizing. The table of contents of books, single-page condensations of school subjects, pamphlet outline series, can all be used to help you better understand how you can make your own summary.

The Art of Outlining

Outlining, like summary writing and mapping, is a learning skill that aids clear thinking, good organization, and the ability to recall more easily what has been learned. The outline is a plan—a blueprint of ideas—and not many solid structures have been built satisfactorily without a plan. The outline does two important things with ideas: (1) It shows the order in which they are arranged. (2) It shows the relative importance of the separate ideas.

The correct outline form is accepted as standard and cannot be varied. The form follows five specific rules: (1) A title is placed at the beginning, but is not numbered or lettered as part of the outline. (2) Roman numerals are used to designate main topics, and they are written to the left of the red margin on lined note-book paper, one inch from the edge of unlined paper, or to the left of the line marking the two-thirds of the page used for your notes. (3) Subtopics are designated in descending order by capital letters, Arabic numerals, then small letters, then Arabic numerals in parentheses, followed by small letters in parentheses. (4)

Subtopics are indented to the right of the main topic, and divisions of the subtopics are indented to the right of the subtopics. All topics of equal rank are in the same column: all main topics in the left margin, subtopics indented from the main topic, divisions of subtopics indented from the subtopics, and so on. When indented, the letter of the subtopic is placed in the space directly under the first letter of the first word of the main topic, the numerals of the divisions of the subtopic are put in the space under the first letter of the first word of the subtopic, and so on. (5) There are always two or more subtopics because subtopics are divisions of the topic above them, and whenever you divide anything, the minimum number of parts is two.

The following examples show correct and incorrect outline form.

Correct Outline Form

Title: The Classical Tradition

I. Greek Poetry
II. Latin Poetry
III. English Poetry
    A. Epic poetry
    B. Lyric poetry
    C. Dramatic poetry
        1. Marlowe's dramatic poetry
        2. Shakespeare's dramatic poetry
            a. Comedies
            b. Tragedies
                (1) *Richard II*
                (2) *Julius Caesar*

Incorrect Outline Form

Title: The Classical Tradition

I. Greek Poetry
    A. Homer's *Iliad*
II. Latin Poetry
    A. Vergil
        1. *Aeneid*
        2. Bucolics

B. Horace
    1. Odes
III. English poetry
  A. Epic poetry
  B. Lyric Poetry
IV. Dramatic poetry
  A. Marlowe's dramatic poetry
  B. Shakespeare's dramatic Poetry
    a. Comedies
    b. Tragedies
  C. *Julius Caesar*
  D. *Richard II*

Notice that in the incorrect form, no proper division has been made of section I. If it had, there would at least be a section B. The same is true of section II B; had there been proper subdividing, in addition to section 1 ("Odes") there would be a section 2. Notice also that section IV contains an error, not so much of form as of logic. Section IV B b bears the title "Tragedies"; logically, *Julius Caesar* and *Richard II,* because they are tragedies, should be included as subdivisions of that topic. Remember, when dividing a topic, you will have at least two parts.

Outlines usually fall into one of several reasonable orders. Items may be arranged logically in (1) Time (chronological) order—such as biography or sequence of events. (2) Numerical order—according to size or number. An outline of coal-producing states would probably start with the one producing the most and go to the one producing the least or vice versa. (3) Alphabetical order—a rather arbitrary order used for convenience. For example, coal-producing states could be outlined alphabetically. (4) Place order—according to location. If one wished to emphasize the regional distribution of coal-producing states, place order could be used.

The key word is *logically,* as it pertains to the purpose of the outline. The arrangement of ideas is a personal matter. The important thing is to have a sensible reason for the arrangement.

The practices of outlining for study and review will usually be no more than the condensation of textbook material. This will not be difficult because most textbooks are arranged in logical patterns of sequence and relationship. As in case of summaries, encyclopedias, especially junior ones, provide excellent models of outlining.

Many good encyclopedias conclude articles that cover two or three pages with an outline of the article. These and your English textbook should afford sufficient examples to help you become expert. Your greatest problem at first will be reducing your outline to sensible proportions. There is always an inclination to include too much.

Examine the sample outline that follows. It is an outline on Chapter 2, on listening. Note the format, especially the highlighting in the left column.

LISTENING: THE EASY WAY TO LEARN

I. Listening is the most difficult of all learning processes.
   A. It must be self taught.
   B. It is hard to discipline yourself to listen.

Hinderances to listening

II. There are four stumbling blocks to good listening.
   A. Listener must coordinate his mind with speaker's.
     1. Listener must not think on tangents.
     2. Listener must accept speaker's ideas, even if he disagrees.
   B. Listener must think at rate speaker speaks.
     1. Listener can think four times faster than speaker can speak.

2. Listener can ponder, briefly, what speaker says, put the ideas into his own words, in order to keep pace.
C. Listener must follow speaker's line of argument even if he disagrees.
D. Listening is not a skill taught in schools.
    1. Most attention is paid to reading.
    2. Listening as a skill is assumed.

Why it pays to listen

III. Much of course material is given orally.
A. In one history course 80 percent of the material was given orally.
B. In science courses even more is given.
C. In language classes 50 percent is given.

How to take notes

IV. Be careful when taking notes from lecture.
A. Be attentive and active.
B. Use proper format.
    1. Divide paper into ⅓–⅔ columns.
    2. Use indenting, spacing, and underlining to emphasize points.
C. Write key ideas.
    1. Do not try to take dictation.
    2. Write in your own words.
D. Do not erase nor copy over.

V. Remember those four suggestions for improving your classroom listening.
A. Be ready with paper and pencil.
B. Make a worksheet.
C. Listen for key words.

VI.

D. Write in your own words.

Avoid these common mistakes when listening.
A. Don't interrupt.
B. Don't be too quick to question.
C. Don't be impatient.
D. Don't make worthless comments.
E. Don't begin to talk by saying, "I think . . ."
F. Don't believe speaking is more important than listening.

Individual Methods of Condensing

Specific advantages are also to be found in condensation practices other than the standard summary and outline. Working notes for review and recall may take several forms. Some students use summary texts. A summary text is a one-sentence statement of a section, chapter, or assignment, recorded daily to give a bird's-eye view of the course at test time. Recitation keys are also useful. They are usually words or phrases written in parallel columns. Sometimes they compare and contrast.

Example:

Mississippi	Amazon
Length:	Length:
Flood season:	Flood season:
Navigation:	Navigation:

Sometimes they merely classify.

Example:

Great Historians	*Great Dramatists*
Herodotus	Aeschylus
Thucydides	Sophocles
Polybius	Euripides

One excellent pattern of recitation key is the multiple column:

Who?	*When?*	*What?*
Darwin	1850	Origin of the Species

Ingenious and helpful methods of condensing can be worked out by each student to satisfy both need and subject. The function of these, however, will not be to replace effective summary writing and outlining. All have a purpose and are invaluable to the student who wants to *remember more, review it in less time, and write it more intelligently on tests.*

Mapping

The third major type of note-taking is mapping. Mapping is drawing a diagram of the information you are condensing.

Many people find it easier to remember pictures than words. These people will find mapping a very good form of note-taking, because it uses their capacity to remember forms and shapes.

You may be someone with a better memory for pictures than for words. Try this simple test. Think of a time in class you had difficulty remembering something you had read. You couldn't remember the information, but you could visualize where it was in your book, perhaps even to the point of identifying what preceded it and what followed it on the page. If you have had such an experience, or numerous such experiences, you will be able to use mapping to good advantage.

To draw a map of a chapter of a text, start with a clean sheet of paper, put the title of your map on the page, and draw a box around it. On our sample of a map, we will put the title in the center of the page. (Our map will be of Chapter 2, on listening.)

> LISTENING:
> the easy way
> to learn

After putting the title on the page, determine the path your eye will follow when reading the map. For our sample map, we have chosen a clockwise path, starting at twelve o'clock.

The third step is to determine the first topic of major importance and to put it on the map, connecting it to the title by a line. On our sample, because the path we have chosen is clockwise, we will put this first major topic at twelve o'clock above the title.

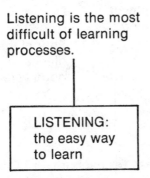

As this major topic subdivides, draw lines from the topic and name them.

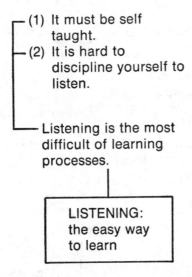

After you have finished the first major topic and all its subdivisions, determine the second major topic and put it next to the first topic, moving according to your chosen eye path. Then as that major topic subdivides, draw lines from the topic and name them.

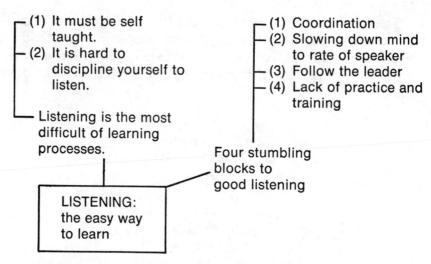

Follow this process for each major topic and its subdivisions, moving around the page in the direction you have chosen.

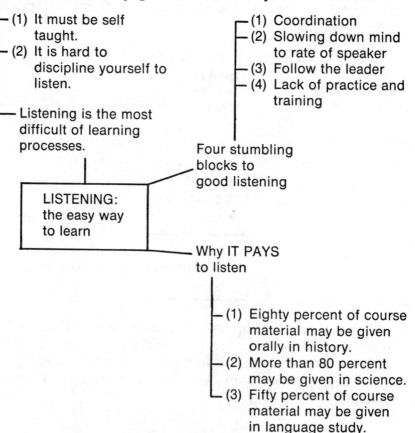

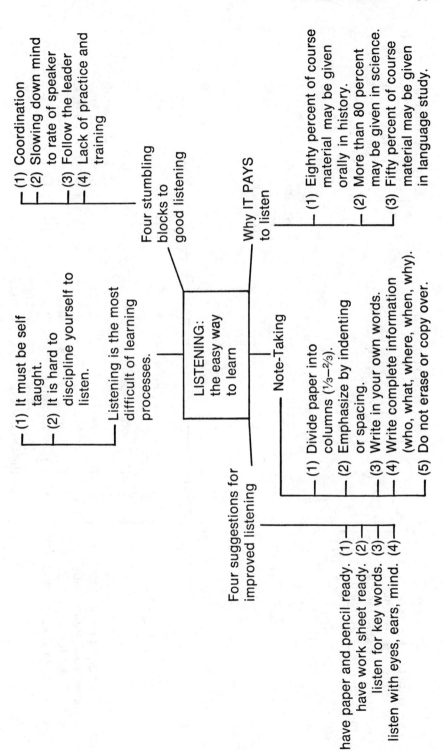

Four stumbling
blocks to
good listening

(1) Coordination
(2) Slowing down mind
    to rate of speaker
(3) Follow the leader
(4) Lack of practice and
    training

Why IT PAYS
to listen

(1) Eighty percent of course
    material may be given
    orally in history.
(2) More than 80 percent
    may be given in science.
(3) Fifty percent of course
    material may be given
    in language study.

(1) It must be self
    taught.
(2) It is hard to
    discipline yourself to
    listen.

Listening is the most
difficult of learning
processes.

LISTENING:
the easy way
to learn

Note-Taking

(1) Divide paper into
    columns (⅓–⅔).
(2) Emphasize by indenting
    or spacing.
(3) Write in your own words.
(4) Write complete information
    (who, what, where, when, why).
(5) Do not erase or copy over.

Four suggestions for
improved listening

have paper and pencil ready. (1)
have work sheet ready. (2)
listen for key words. (3)
listen with eyes, ears, mind. (4)

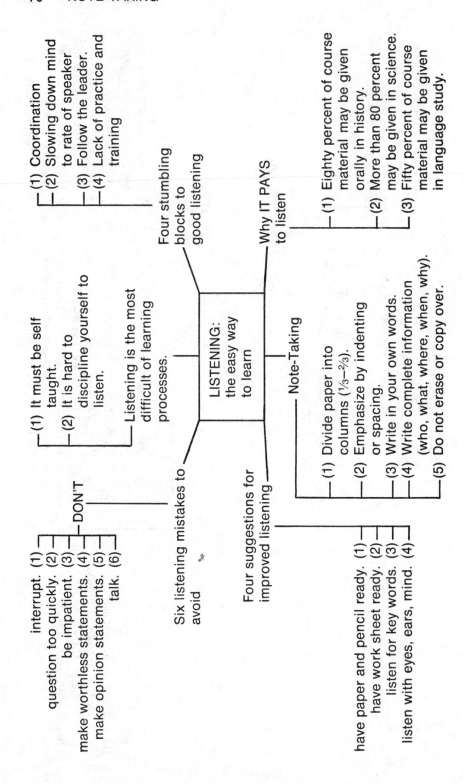

LISTENING: the easy way to learn

Four stumbling blocks to good listening
(1) Coordination
(2) Slowing down mind to rate of speaker
(3) Follow the leader.
(4) Lack of practice and training

Why IT PAYS to listen
(1) Eighty percent of course material may be given orally in history.
(2) More than 80 percent may be given in science.
(3) Fifty percent of course material may be given in language study.

Listening is the most difficult of learning processes.
(1) It must be self taught.
(2) It is hard to discipline yourself to listen.

Six listening mistakes to avoid — DON'T
(1) interrupt.
(2) question too quickly.
(3) be impatient.
(4) make worthless statements.
(5) make opinion statements.
(6) talk.

Note-Taking
(1) Divide paper into columns (⅓–⅔).
(2) Emphasize by indenting or spacing.
(3) Write in your own words.
(4) Write complete information (who, what, where, when, why).
(5) Do not erase or copy over.

Four suggestions for improved listening
(1) have paper and pencil ready.
(2) have work sheet ready.
(3) listen for key words.
(4) listen with eyes, ears, mind.

Our map of Chapter 2 reaches its final form with the addition of the sixth major topic and its subdivisions (see page 70).

Mapping may take any form you wish—feel free to use whatever shapes you find make sense to you. You may use colors to code the areas, or you may use any eye path that is comfortable for you. On page 72 is another map of Chapter 2, using a different eye path. Read this one from left to right. Which of the maps is easier for you to use?

You need not make such spidery things as our sample maps. Many people have great success using overlapping circles or geometric shapes—triangles for three part ideas, squares for four, and so on. The only object of a map is to present information clearly to you, so that you can understand and remember easily what you have read.

Mapping may be used for notes from lectures as well as for notes from reading. Try this type of note-taking, particularly if you have a good visual memory. With a little practice, you will find that it can be very helpful.

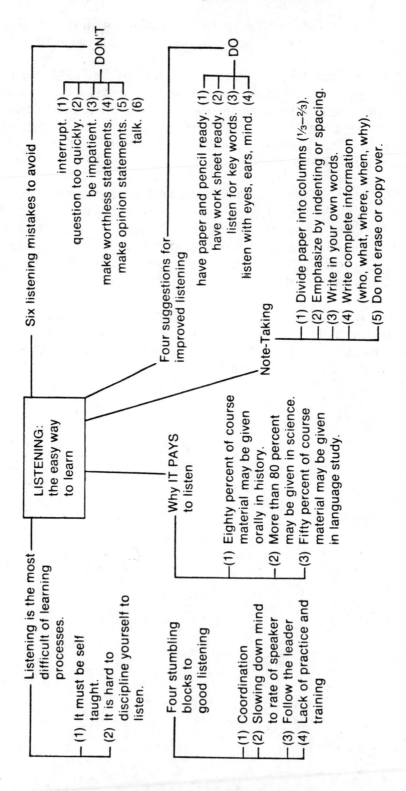

LISTENING:
the easy way
to learn

Listening is the most difficult of learning processes.
(1) It must be self taught.
(2) It is hard to discipline yourself to listen.

Six listening mistakes to avoid
(1) interrupt.
(2) question too quickly.
(3) be impatient.
(4) make worthless statements.
(5) make opinion statements.
(6) talk.
— DON'T

Four suggestions for improved listening
(1) have paper and pencil ready.
(2) have work sheet ready.
(3) listen for key words.
(4) listen with eyes, ears, mind.
— DO

Note-Taking
(1) Divide paper into columns (⅓–⅔).
(2) Emphasize by indenting or spacing.
(3) Write in your own words.
(4) Write complete information (who, what, where, when, why).
(5) Do not erase or copy over.

Why IT PAYS to listen
(1) Eighty percent of course material may be given orally in history.
(2) More than 80 percent may be given in science.
(3) Fifty percent of course material may be given in language study.

Four stumbling blocks to good listening
(1) Coordination
(2) Slowing down mind to rate of speaker
(3) Follow the leader
(4) Lack of practice and training

Suggestions for Better Summary Writing

1. Read and study with summary intent. Practice conditioning your mind to summarize. Use pleasure reading—newspapers, magazines, novels—as training ground. Visualize as you study work-type reading—textbooks, etc.—the pattern of unity you would use for a summary answer.

2. Train yourself to replace the author's words with your own, but not just an equivalent word. Try to select an equally impressive synonym or a better one. This makes your summary so personal that recall is almost automatic.

3. Practice economy of words. Link parallel details together. Use the semicolon to emphasize in one sentence what is expressed in the original text in three. Learn to link ideas in series for easy recall. Practicing economy of words is an aid to separating main points from nonessential introductory and illustrative material.

4. Avoid generalization, unnecessary lead-ins, and double conclusions. Learn to distinguish between opinion and fact. If you are writing about Washington at Valley Forge, it is probably unwise to start by reminding your teacher that Washington was the commander-in-chief of the Continental Army. You need not repeat, in a last dangling sentence, the fact that Washington had a trying winter at Valley Forge; that's what you have just finished summarizing.

5. Learn to distinguish between fragmentation and summarization. Fragmentation is bringing together ideas from an assignment and recording them in a haphazard manner. A good summary is a miniature theme containing all the elements—unity, coherence, and emphasis.

6. Do not content yourself with reading one or two summaries and accepting them as models. Compare the summaries you write with ones on similar topics in encyclopedias. The reference shelf in a library is a good storehouse of models.

7. When you write your summaries, make sure that you follow the ⅓–⅔ format on the page, saving the left-hand column for highlighting when you review your notes.

Suggestions for Better Outlines

1. Observe carefully the standard outline form. Any change, transposition, or incorrect indentation is evidence of disregard for order and accepted authority.

2. Avoid the most common error in outlining—leaving off the title or designating it as a main topic.

3. Be sure your outline performs two functions: (1) the arrangement of ideas; and (2) the relative importance of the ideas.

4. Remember that a subtopic results from division of a topic. Therefore, there will always be at least two subtopics—*A* and *B*, *1* and *2*, *a* and *b*. Nothing that is divided can remain whole (one); it will become two, three, etc., depending upon its separate parts.

5. Know the orders of outlines: (1) time, (2) numerical, (3) alphabetical, and (4) place. With each, use the key word *logical* to give ideas the most sensible arrangement. If you can reasonably explain your arrangement, your outline is probably in good order.

6. Use the outline as an aid to memory, a blueprint for easy recall, an organizational frame for written tests and themes, and a time-saver at examination time. The only

students who get their money's worth from textbooks are those who develop outlining into a regular and efficient study skill.

7. Make sure to use the ⅓–⅔ format for your outline, leaving the left-hand column for highlighting when you review.

Suggestions for Better Mapping

1. Have a clear idea of the form your map will take. For example, will it contain radiating lines, or will it look like a wall of building blocks?

2. Use shapes that are meaningful—triangles are good for three-part ideas, concentric circles for sets and subsets, octagons for things not to do, since we associate that shape with stop signs.

3. Use color coding if you can—one topic completely in blue, another in red, another in black, and so forth.

4. Make sure the units of the map are distinct and clearly separated from one another.

5. Write the words so that you need not rotate the paper to read them.

Looking Back

1. These social studies notes were found in a high-school
    student's notebook. They deal with a lesson on Mao
    Tse-tung, the powerful Chinese leader of post-World
    War II. As you examine them, point out (a) their
    strengths, (b) their weaknesses; then suggest ways in
    which the notes could be improved.

World History 104   _February 9_

Mao Tse-tung

- ambitious for country's growth
- looked in four different directions: Korea, Vietnam, Tibet
                                                Nationalist China
- North Korea / U.S.
- Foothold after Armistice
- Mao was a veritable thorn in the side of the United
    States when it came to Vietnam. He sent arms,
    soldiers, and officers to help the Communist
    Vietnamese combat the French and then the
    United States.
- Tibet conquest - gateway India
- First "protect"
- Attack religion
- Takeover followed
- Taiwan ever since 1949
- American fleet a headache

2. One of your classmates says: "Mr. Reardon always asks for an outline along with our English compositions. I write the composition first, then make up the outline for old Reardon. He never gets wise to my short cut!"

    How good is that technique? Before you answer, try it out both ways—writing the outline before and after you do your next writing assignment.

7

SPELLING AND PUNCTUATION: HALLMARKS OF EXCELLENCE

True Confessions

1. "When I was in elementary school," a famous novelist said, "I used to throw up out of fear every Friday morning because that was the day for the weekly spelling test."

   Why might a spelling test hold such terrors for a student? Are you confident about your spelling ability? Are you embarrassed by spelling errors you make?

2. "I think it's foolish to waste so much time on spelling. Today we have word processing machines and electronic gadgets of all kinds that can correct our mistakes for us."

   What is your opinion of this student's statement?

3. "Marge," said Joan, "is a pinhead."
   "Marge said Joan is a pinhead."

   Who is the pinhead? What important observation regarding punctuation can we make from examining these two short sentences?

Hallmarks of Quality

What is all your work going to accomplish if you can't spell accurately? Now that you have worked hard to plan your time, master your assignments, and take notes, finish the job by polishing your spelling and punctuation. A fine piece of silver bears the hallmark *sterling* on its base to show that it is made of materials of quality. Let your accurate spelling and flawless punctuation be the hallmarks of quality in your work.

General Spelling Faults and How to Correct Them

Many poor spellers make most of their mistakes by misspelling a few words repeatedly. If you find yourself burdened by this kind of faulty spelling, you can remedy your problem quickly if you are willing to work at it.

First, keep a list of words you misspell most frequently. When you add a word to the list, illuminate the part of the word you misspell by capitalizing the letters you miss most often.

apitude	apTitude
seperate	sepArate
privelege	privIlege
litrature	litErature
Febuary	FebRuary
boundry	boundAry
ocassionaly	oCCaSionaLLy

Second, go over this list orally from time to time. Then close your eyes, and visualize the trouble spots in capital letters. Open your eyes, and repeat the list; then close them, and visualize the word in small letters, as they would appear on the printed page. Then write the list correctly several times.

Most poor spellers also are careless in what they write. If you find yourself transposing letters or omitting them and can recognize the errors when you reread your work, you will improve your spelling by becoming more careful, by thinking about spelling as you write. You may also correct this kind of error by keeping a list of words you commonly misspell through carelessness. Head the list *Unnecessary Mistakes*, review it a few times, just as you do with your other spelling errors, and you will no longer misspell those words on the list.

Some poor spellers fall into error because they do not pronounce words correctly and add or omit syllables. Some people disregard pronunciation keys in the dictionary, even when they look up words; others never audibly sound out a word they are trying to spell.

You will find that pronouncing words carefully and correctly will help your spelling, even though many English words are not spelled phonetically (according to sound). You may find it helpful to underline the syllables you add or omit.

labratory	laboratory
practicly	practically
disasterous	disastrous
rememberance	remembrance
hinderance	hindrance
enterance	entrance
intrest	interest

Other poor spellers have difficulty with homonyms. "Homonym" comes from the Greek words *homos*, meaning same, and *onoma*, meaning name—thus, "homonym" means same name. Homonyms are words that have the same name (sound) but different meaning and spelling, such as *to, too, two—right, write, rite, wright—you, yew, ewe—*and *pair, pare, pear.*

You can correct this all too common spelling fault by learning homonyms and their meanings. Some of the ones most often misused follow:

aloud	altogether	all ready
allowed	all together	already
alter	assent	advise
altar	ascent	advice
bare	birth	born
bear	berth	borne
bow	break	by
bough	brake	buy
canon	capitol	coarse
cannon	capital	course
corps	compliment	council
corpse	complement	counsel
decent	dual	desert
descent	duel	dessert
dear	fair	forth
deer	fare	fourth
goal	grown	hear
gold	groan	here
heir	heal	him
air	heel	hymn
hole	herd	knew
whole	heard	new
lesson	led	meat
lessen	lead (metal)	meet
made	mist	pail
maid	missed	pale
peace	peal	plain
piece	peel	plane
pour	principal	profit
pore	principle	prophet

seam	shown	steal
seem	shone	steel
steak	stationary	son
stake	stationery	sun
tale	their	to
tail	there	too
	they're	two
threw	write	weather
through	right	whether
	rite	

Syllables and Sound in Correct Spelling

As you work to overcome your spelling errors, you can make your job easier if you learn thoroughly the basic rules for division of words into syllables, if you have a sense of phonetics, and if you know basic spelling rules. The person who always has to check a dictionary to find how a plural is formed, when a *y* changes to an *i*, or when an *e* is dropped before a suffix, spends an untold amount of valuable time on something that he can learn for all time if only he will study a little.

Syllables are parts of words that make one sound unit. The word *syllable* comes from Greek and means *to take together*. Thus, the letters that make up a syllable are taken together to form a sound unit.

The six rules for division of words into syllables that follow should be part of your everyday working knowledge.

1.   There are as many syllables in a word as there are vowels, except when two vowels are sounded as one or when the final *e* is silent. (In English there are many exceptions to rules, but careful observation can make the exception as familiar as the rule). The vowel sounds are *a, e, i, o, u,* and *y* when it is sounded as *i*.

Examples of Rule 1:
vocabulary, vo-cab-u-lar-y
dictionary, dic-tion-ar-y (*io* is one sound)
atmosphere, at-mos-phere (the final *e* is silent)
Two vowels making one sound: d*oe*s, l*oo*k, m*ea*n, r*ai*l, scr*ea*m
Silent *e* at the end of a word: alon*e*, glu*e*, hemispher*e*, improv*e*, hom*e*

2. If two consonants come between two vowels, the syllable division is usually between the consonants. (Consonants are all the letters of the alphabet that are not vowels.)

   Examples for Rule 2:
   Mon-day, Tues-day, plun-der, pen-cil, may-be

3. When a consonant occurs between two vowels, the consonant goes with the second vowel unless the word is accented on the first syllable.

   Examples of Rule 3:
   be-fore, pri-mate, ar-bor, pa-per, va-cant
   Examples of first syllable accent:
   vow-el, med-al, vol-ume, mod-el, giv-er

4. Words ending in *le* with a consonant before the *le* keep the consonant with the *le*, except for the consonant *k*.

   Examples of Rule 4:
   cir-cle, pur-ple, Bi-ble, un-cle, ea-gle
   Examples of *le* words with *k*:
   tack-le, pick-le, fick-le, buck-le, chuck-le

5. Double consonants are always split in syllable division.

   Examples of Rule 5:
   col-lege, pil-low, sil-ly, mid-day, let-ter

6. Prefixes and suffixes remain separate syllables when added to words, except *ed* unless it follows *t* or *d*.

   Examples of Rule 6:
   en-close, re-cover, final-ly, hope-ful, mean-ness
   Examples of *ed* *not* a separate syllable:
   resign*ed*, cook*ed*, stepp*ed*, climb*ed*, fill*ed*

Examples of *ed as* a separate syllable:
test-ed, dat-ed, plant-ed, collid-ed, prod-ded

Perhaps the exceptions in the rules noted above give you cause to wonder. Pronunciation provides the key; how the words sound as they are spoken determines syllable division. For example, look at Rule 6 above. *Ed* is a separate syllable in test*ed* because the word is pronounced as two syllables, test-ed. Were the *ed* in cook*ed* a separate syllable, the word would have to be pronounced cook-ed. Instead the word is pronounced "cookt," and so the *ed*-suffix is not a separate syllable.

Your dictionary provides you with phonetic spellings and accent marks as keys to pronunciation. Study them, and learn how to use them. Pay attention to the sounds of vowels and diphthongs. Diphthongs are two vowels that combine to make one sound, as the *ai* in the word br*ai*n. Look up the following terms in your dictionary, and remember what each is: breve, macron, schwa, diacritical, and digraph.

Spelling Rules and Exceptions

The rules of spelling that follow will aid you in developing proper habits and establishing certain correct patterns:

1. Words that contain *ei* and *ie* follow a two-part rule.
    (a) Write *i* before *e* except after *c*.

    Examples:

ie	ei
bel*ie*ve	rece*i*ve
rel*ie*f	rece*i*pt
ach*ie*ve	ce*i*ling

    (b) Write *ei* when the sound is *a*. Examples: weigh (way), neighbor (nā-ber), freight (frāt). Some exceptions are: either, weird, leisure, seize, protein.

2. When a suffix beginning with a vowel (able, ance, ed, ing, ist) is added, double the final consonant if the consonant is preceded by a single vowel that is accented.

    Examples:

begi*nn*ing	acqui*tt*ed
refe*rr*ing	occu*rr*ed
commi*tt*ed	occu*rr*ence
expe*ll*ed	allo*tt*ed
dru*gg*ist	swi*mm*ing

    Exceptions occur when the suffix changes the accent. Examples: transfe*rr*ed (transfe*r*able), prefe*rr*ing (pref*er*ence), refe*rr*ed (ref*er*ence). Exceptions also result from alternate accepted spellings.
    Examples: trave*l*ing (trave*ll*ing), worshi*p*ing (worshi*pp*ing), paralle*l*ed (paralle*ll*ed).

3. Words that end in a silent *e* drop the *e* if a suffix beginning with a vowel is added.

    Examples:

come—coming	dine—dining
desire—desirable	force—forcing
believe—believable	debate—debating

    Exceptions occur in words ending in *ce* and *ge* when the suffix begins with *a* or *o*. Examples: peaceable, noticeable, courageous, serviceable. Exceptions also occur with some words ending in *e* when the suffix begins with a consonant.
    Examples: whole (wholly), true (truly), awe (awful), judge (judgment).

4. Words that end in *y* after a consonant change the *y* to *i* when suffixes are added, except when those suffixes begin with *i*.

    Examples:

try—tries	carry—carries
dry—dries	apply—applies
vary—varied	notify—notified

    Examples of suffix beginning with *i*: try—trying, rely—relying, worry—worrying, dry—drying, pity—pitying.

5. Words ending in *y* change the *y* to *i* for the *ly* suffix; those ending in *e*, except *le*, also add *ly*.

*Examples of **y** to **i:***

lazy—lazily	merry—merrily
temporary—temporarily	steady—steadily
satisfactory—satisfactorily	ordinary—ordinarily
late—lately	extreme—extremely
sincere—sincerely	definite—definitely

Exceptions occur when words end in *le*. The *e* is dropped and *y* added:

Examples:

able—ably	gentle—gently
audible—audibly	subtle—subtly
reliable—reliably	double—doubly

6. Words ending in *l* add *ly*.

Examples:

personal—personally	hopeful—hopefully
usual—usually	cruel—cruelly
awful—awfully	oral—orally

Spelling Demons

There are other rules and other exceptions, but this half dozen will help you form better habits of spelling.

The New York Board of Regents has prepared a list of words often misspelled by high-school students. As you study them, visualize how they are most frequently misspelled.

SIMPLE WORDS OFTEN MISSPELLED

ache	any	break (to shatter)
again	been	built
always	beginning	business
among	believe	busy
answer	blue	buy

can't
choose (present
   tense; *chose* is
   past tense)
color
coming
cough
could
country
dear
doctor
does
done
don't
early
easy
enough
every
February
forty
friend
grammar

guess
half
having
hear (ear)
heard
here (*there*—a
   place)
hoarse (frog in your
   throat)
hour
instead
just
knew
know
laid
loose (adjective and
   verb)
lose (verb—to *lose*
   money)
making
many

meant
minute
much
none
often
once
piece (a part of
   something)
raise
read (spelling is
   same for all
   tenses)
ready
said
says
seems
separate
shepherd
shoes
since
some

Make a list of your own, starting with spelling demons from the preceding selection. Add words you commonly misspell until you have reached three hundred. If you master your troublesome list of three hundred, you will probably be a better than average speller for the rest of your life. You will have evaluated your faults and developed habits to correct them.

When you have compiled your own list of three hundred, compare it with the following. The spelling demons that follow were misspelled most often on papers in a five-year test conducted at Kent School, Kent, Connecticut.

absence
accidentally
accommodate
accumulate
achievement
acknowledge
acquaintance
across

advice (noun)
advise (verb)
aggravate
all right
altogether
always
among
analysis

apparent
appearance
appropriate
arctic
argument
arrangement
ascend
assistant

association
athletics
audience
auxiliary
awful
awkward

beautiful
beginning
believe
benefit
boundary
breathe
bureau
business

calendar
campaign
candidate
captain
cemetery
certain
changeable
college
coming
committee
comparatively
completely
conceive
conquer
conscience
conscious
convenience
convenient
copies
courageous
courteous
criticism
criticize
crowd
curiosity

defense
definite

describe
description
desirable
despair
desperate
develop
dining
disappear
disappoint
disastrous
discipline
disease
dissatisfied
divide
doctor
doesn't

ectasy
efficient
eighth
embarrass
equipped
especially
exaggerate
excellent
exercise
exhaust
existence
explanation
extraordinary

familiar
fascinate
fatigue
February
finally
foreign
forty
fourth
friend
fulfill

generally
genius

government
governor
grammar
grateful
grievous
guarantee
guard
guardian
gymnasium

handkerchief
harass
height
heroes
hindrance
hoping
horizon
hospital
hurriedly
hypocrisy

imagination
immediately
incidentally
independent
indispensable
infinite
initial
instance
intelligence
interest
interpret
irresistible
its

judgment

knowledge

laboratory
leisure
liable
license
lightning
likely

literature
loneliness
lonely
lose
lying

maintain
maintenance
maneuver
manual
marriage
mathematics
meant
medicine
medieval
merely
miniature
minimum
minute
mischievous
misspelled
movable
muscle
mysterious

necessary
necessity
neither
nickel
niece
nineteen
ninety
ninth
noticeable
nuisance

obedience
occasion
occasionally
occurred
occurrence
omission
omitted
opinion

opportunity
optimism
optimistic
orchestra
original
outrageous

pamphlet
parallel
parliament
particularly
pastime
peaceable
perceive
perform
perhaps
permanent
permissible
personally
personnel
perspiration
persuade
physician
picnic
planning
portrait
portray
possess
possibility
practically
preceding
preferred
prejudice
privilege
probably
procedure
proceed
professor
pronunciation
purpose
pursue

quantity

quiet
quite

realize
really
receive
recognize
recommend
referred
reign
relief
religious
repetition
representative
restaurant
rhythm
ridiculous
roommate

safety
satisfactorily
schedule
secretary
seize
sentence
separate
shining
siege
similar
sincerely
sophomore
specimen
speech
strength
strenuous
stretch
studying
subtle
succeed
success
successful
sufficient
supersede

superior
surely
surprise
syllable

tariff
temperament
thorough
thoroughly
tragedy
tremendous
truly
tyranny

Tuesday
twelfth

unanimous
undoubtedly
unnecessary
until
usually

vacuum
varieties
vegetable

vengeance
vicinity
villain

Wednesday
weird
welfare
wherever
wholly
women
writing
written

Summary of Practices for Spelling Mastery

1. By self-examination find the few words you misspell again and again. Make a list of them, and check it until you can recognize each troublemaker at a glance.

2. Correct the spelling fault of omitting, adding, and transposing letters in simple words by looking at the word. Many of the easiest words are misspelled because you have really never seen them.

3. Study pronunciation marks when you use the dictionary, and form the habit of pronouncing words correctly. Pronounce all new words several times. Write them by syllable division, consulting your dictionary if necessary.

4. Keep a handy list of the most confusing homonyms. Use it to avoid incorrect usage. Know the basic rules of spelling, and keep one or two examples in mind.

5. Know the basic rules for dividing words into syllables, the vowel sounds, and the diacritical marks. Keep in

mind two or three examples of each rule for syllable division.

6. Keep you own list of spelling demons. Study the list of simple words most often misspelled. Compare your own list of troublesome words with other lists. Note your weaknesses by checking the type of mistake you make: is it the *ei—ie* word, is it the *ly* suffix, is it the dropped *e*? Locate your specific weakness and correct it. Conscious awareness is often more than half the remedy.

The final word on spelling is *vision*. There are so many exceptions to rule and sound in English that perhaps a sense of keen perception is the one best practice in becoming a proficient speller. People gifted with photographic minds, that is, with the visual mindedness to recall what a page looks like, what is on it, etc., seem to be generally the best spellers. Then perhaps to *see critically* is to *succeed*.

The Function of Punctuation

Something of the history, nature, and usage regarding punctuation seems likely to be both more interesting and profitable. The basic rules you must know; these are your primary responsibility. Here we will concern ourselves with proper interpretation of the rules so as to make punctuation something less arbitrary and more personal and meaningful.

The function of punctuation is to "slow down" or "stop." The word *punctuation* comes from the Latin word *punctus*, meaning a point. Thus, the differently shaped points (marks) of punctuation keep words from running away. In the "slowing" and "stopping" process, marks of punctuation replace gesture, changes of voice, pauses, and changes of thought.

Punctuation usage has changed much over the centuries. People used to read everything aloud, so punctuation maintained a closer control than is necessary for rapid, silent reading. As people learned to read silently, see more words at an eye fixation, punctuation did not need to control as strictly. Today modern writers use less punctuation than was the custom a hundred years ago. Editors and generally accepted usage have established rules that are recognized as standard. At the same time punctuation usage is flexible enough to be personal to a degree. Whether you use close or loose punctuation is not of first importance. First you must learn the rules that will give you the foundation of knowledge needed in order to make the proper judgments for effective control and relationship of words.[1]

The Characteristics of the Marks of Punctuation

An understanding of the general nature or characteristics of the several marks of punctuation that are not self-explanatory, such as interrogation (question), exclamatory, and quotation marks, can add meaning to the rules of usage. The character of the *period* is to indicate a full stop. It implies a pause at the end of a unit of thought standing alone.

Related to it is the *semicolon,* whose nature is to indicate a "slowing down" between coordinate elements within a sentence—two clauses (related or parallel thoughts). The "slowing down" indicated by the semicolon may be compared to the slowing down of a car for the yellow traffic signal between the red and the green.

The *comma* is related to the semicolon in that it is a pause. However, it is much weaker, resembling in many respects a blinking caution light, which demands less "slowing down." *Parentheses* and the *dash* sometimes replace the comma in setting off added words or ideas (called parenthetical material). The

---

1. Adapted from *The Tools of Thinking: A Workbook*, William H. Armstrong. Barron's Educational Series. 1965.

writer is given certain freedoms in the use of each to achieve emphasis, variety, and to suit different conditions.

The nature of the *colon* is to indicate that something important is being introduced: (1) a significant explanation, (2) a long quotation, or (3) a list which may be words or groups of words.

One of the simplest of all the marks of punctuation is the apostrophe. Its uses are to show *possession* (John, John's; somebody, somebody's; Caesar, Caesar's); the *omission of letters* in words (doesn't, can't, won't, couldn't); and the *plural of numbers,* letters, words, and symbols (1960's, 1880's, 6's, k's, p's, m's, too's, and's, but's, M.D.'s, G.I.'s, V.I.P.'s). The apostrophe is, strangely, the most neglected of all punctuation. Can it be that its uses are so easy they are thought unimportant? Be sure that your written work is not marked CARELESS because you ignore the apostrophe. It is just as important as any other mark of punctuation.

With a knowledge of rules and an understanding of the nature of punctuation, you should have no difficulty choosing, where choice is allowed, to suit your own style of writing and distinctive conditions. In an essay entitled *Guide to Usage,* Harrison Platt, Jr., gives a wonderful bit of advice that seems most fitting and proper for the conclusion of any discussion of punctuation. "If a sentence is very difficult to punctuate," he writes, "so as to make the meaning clear, the chances are that the arrangement of words and ideas is at fault. The writer will do better if he rearranges his word order instead of wrestling with his punctuation."[2] To have this advice and use it is to possess a treasure.

Summary of Enlightened Punctuation

1. Appreciate the basic function of punctuation—to give your written word its final clarification.

2. Harrison Platt, Jr., "Guide to Usage," The *American College Dictionary* (New York: Random House, 1969), 1455.

2. Know the rules that govern the use of punctuation marks.

3. Add interest to what might seem a rather drab study by knowing something of the history and development of punctuation.

4. Know the nature and general character of the several punctuation marks, particularly those that perform related functions.

5. Use the freedom allowed the writer, within the rules, in order that punctuation may be personal and a part of the individual style in writing.

6. And remember always—if punctuation cannot clarify, change the word arrangement.

Looking Back

1. One of the suggestions for becoming a better speller is that you keep a list of the words you commonly misspell. What two additional suggestions for improving your spelling did you find in this chapter?

2.   THINK A-
                HEAD

    Although the sign maker divided the word *ahead* properly into two syllables, the awkwardness of his message shows that he didn't think ahead. What advice could you have given him?

3. Most people remember the *ie*, *ei* rule by saying "*i* before *e*, except after *c*, or when as pronounced *ay*, as in neighbor or weigh."

    Make up a similar jingle for any of the other spelling rules in this chapter.

4. Insert the five punctuation marks referred to in this

chapter (period, semicolon, colon, comma, apostrophe) where they belong in the following sentence:

The store detectives boss gave him the following orders mingle with the crowds keep your eyes open for people with large bags be alert he promised he would do his best.

8

STUDYING FOR SUBJECTS: ADAPTING YOUR METHODS TO THE SUBJECT

True Confessions

1. The major subject areas in high school are English, social studies, mathematics, science, and foreign languages. Which of those areas give you the most trouble? Explain the reasons for your difficulty.

2. The chapter you are about to read contains practical study tips that can help you do better in those subjects. If you were writing the chapter, what important study tip would you list for each of those major subjects?

3. When Mrs. Green met her son's geometry teacher on Open-School Night, she was told that her boy had a defeatist attitude and expected to fail. Mrs. Green replied, "I'm not surprised he is doing poorly in your subject, because both my husband and I were weak math students in school."

   How should the teacher have responded to that comment?

Method Plus Work Equals Success

To give the reason for their failure in academic subjects, some people claim a lack of aptitude for the subjects, saying they just cannot learn mathematics or foreign languages (to name two of the most commonly quoted subjects). While it is true that some people have such low aptitudes for certain subjects as to prevent their success, most people can overcome low aptitude by hard work. Most failure in school subjects comes from failure to study enough or to study in a proper way.

Thus, your habits of work will be significant factors in determining the grades you earn. All your knowledge about time planning, study methods, note-taking, and spelling will be of little use unless you put that knowledge to work. For every subject, you will need to make minor adaptations in your study method so as to emphasize the areas of the subject in which you need to concentrate most of your efforts.

Foreign Languages

Studying foreign languages requires that you learn the vocabulary, pronunciation, and grammar of a language different to one degree or another from your native tongue. In studying a modern language, such as French or German, you will learn to read, write, hear, and speak the language; while in studying an ancient language, such as Greek or Latin, you will be asked to learn to read and write, but usually not be asked to converse in the language.

The major areas of study will be vocabulary building; learning the forms (morphology) of adjectives, nouns, and verbs; learning the rules of grammar; practice in hearing and speaking, and reading and translating.

Memorization is the key to learning vocabulary and forms. The first step in memorizing is to determine what it is that you need to learn; the teacher or textbook will probably be specific about this. The next step is for you to write down what you need to know in a form that is easy to use. For vocabulary building write the words on cards, the word on one side, the English definition on the other; or write the words and their definitions in parallel columns on notebook paper, one column in the left margin and one in the right. (That way you will not be able to see both columns at the same time.)

For building your knowledge of forms write them in charts:

PERSON	SINGULAR	PLURAL	
1	sum	sumus	Present tense of the latin verb *sum, esse, fui, futurus*
2	es	estis	
3	est	sunt	

The verb *to be*

	SINGULAR	PLURAL	
Nominative	dux	duces	Declension of third declension noun
Genitive	ducis	ducum	
Dative	duci	ducibus	
Accusative	ducem	duces	
Ablative	duce	ducibus	

The noun *Leader*

The third step in memory work is to recite *out loud* the whole stack of cards, list, or chart until you can recite them perfectly without looking. In the case of a list, start by breaking the list up into small groups, seven items to a group; learn the first group, then go on to the second. When you have learned the second, go back over the first and second together; then proceed to the third group, and so on, until you have learned the whole list or chart. Then put the list aside, and after eight to twenty-four hours, review the list *out loud*, again in the small groups, until you can recite the list perfectly once more without looking. The best time for such recitation and review is immediately before going to bed and upon awaking. It seems that your mind continues to review the list while you sleep! The fourth step is once again to review orally the material to be learned within two days, and then within seven days. If you follow this procedure, you will never forget what you have memorized.

Oral recitation also plays an important role in learning grammar. Make sure you understand *exactly* what the rules of grammar are that you are being asked to learn. Then as you study, recite them *out loud* until you have learned them. Make sure to use them. You will lose your knowledge of the rules if you don't use them. It is also helpful to compare and contrast the rules of grammar of a foreign language with the rules of grammar for English.

Practice in hearing and speaking will develop your oral command of the language. Pay attention to your teachers, listen carefully to their pronunciation, and imitate their speech. Pay attention to your fellow students; as they recite, recite silently along with them, note their errors and the teachers' corrections.

Reading and translating are two similar but distinct skills. Both require the student to understand what a passage says and means. To translate, the student must be able to write accurately in English what the passage says. To read, the student must understand, in the language itself, what a passage says. Fortunately, the same study techniques improve both skills. Read phrase by phrase rather than word by word, and guess at the vocabulary from context before looking up new words in a dictionary. Keep lists of words and idiomatic expressions you had to look up three or more times, and memorize them. There are also three practices that hinder the development of skill in a foreign language. Avoid these three as much as you can. Avoid writing full translations (unless your teacher requires them), avoid writing between the lines of your text, and avoid using published translations to help you understand a passage.

Hints for Language Study

1. Imitate fluent speakers as much as you can. Imitate your teacher and use the language laboratory if your school has one.

2. Memorize rules of grammar, vocabulary, and forms until you know them and can recall them accurately.

3. Study *out loud* as much as you can.

4. Space your studying effectively. Break assignments up into small units, and review after every two or three units. Break your study time into periods of about twenty minutes. After each period, take a five-minute break from hard studying, to review quickly or even to get up and move around a bit.

5. *Study every day.* When you are learning a foreign language, you are embarking on a journey through an unknown wilderness—your teacher is your guide, your text is your guide. If you don't study every day, you won't keep up with your guides, and you will get lost.

English

The study of English includes three distinct areas: grammar, literature, and composition. While these areas are distinct, they are closely connected; and what you learn in one area you may apply in the others.

Grammar

Grammar is the standardized set of rules by which one composes sentences in order to communicate. Most of the fundamental rules you have been acquiring since you first began to talk, and have learned well. In school you will polish your knowledge of grammar, learning not only how to identify these fundamental rules, but also learning additional rules—the intricate rules of clear, forceful expression.

The study of grammar involves a special terminology that you must learn thoroughly if you are to be successful. This terminology describes words and how words are used. Traditional terms that describe words are: noun, verb, adjective, adverb, preposition, and so on. Traditional terms that describe how words are used are: subject, direct object, indirect object, object of a preposition, appositive, and so on.

The grammar textbook that you use in school may be of the traditional sort and use such terms as these, or it may not follow tradition and use terms different from these to describe what is going on in sentences. Regardless of the style, it will use terminology to name the functions of words and parts of sentences; and it is in your best interest to make sure you know what those terms are and what they mean.

The best way to learn these terms is to memorize them thoroughly so as to make them forever a part of your education. In your notebook, make flashcards or lists of these terms, and use the cards or lists in the ways mentioned above in the section of this chapter dealing with foreign language study.

In addition to memorizing the terms of grammar, you will need to learn the rules governing the use of words. Your textbook and your teacher will provide you with a few sample sentences illustrating the rules as you study them in class. Make sure that you understand each rule and that you see how the samples illustrate the rule; ask your teacher for help if you do not. Devote a special section of your English notebook to the rules of grammar, and add your own sample sentences to the ones your teacher and text have given you. Last and perhaps most important, keep at your study of grammar until you can explain any sentence you see. Then check up on yourself from time to time to keep your knowledge current.

Literature

In the study of English, you also will be asked to examine literature closely. Most of your time will be spent on fiction, but you also will read poetry, drama, essays, and, perhaps, some forms of history, such as biography and cultural history. As you read a work of literature, you will be asked to know *what* the author has written, *how* the author has written it, and what *your response* has been to it.

As tools to express ideas about how authors write, your teachers and texts will use terms of literary criticism. As with every other academic discipline, it is in your best interests to learn this specialized vocabulary; and, as before, the best way is through flashcards or lists in a special section of your English notebook. Pay careful attention in class when your teacher talks about terms such as *irony, tone, theme, plot, symbol,* and *figures of speech.* Make notes in your notebook explaining these kinds of terms and citing specific references to the work you are then reading. If you own the book you are reading, put notes in the margins.

Below are worksheets to use as you read different kinds of literature. Use them *before you read* to help your mind get set for reading critically, *while you read* to help you take notes, and *after you have read* to organize your review for tests.

WORKSHEET FOR A NOVEL

1. Who is the author? When and where did the author live? Knowing the historical and cultural context in which an author lived will help you understand the novel.
2. What is the title of the novel? Does it make you think of anything?
3. Who are the major and minor characters? Are they realistic? Why might the author not use realistic characters?
4. How does the author tell the story? For example, is the story told chronologically, in the third person, in the first person? Is the story one of action, or one of reflection, or of feelings? Does the author use foreshadowing or flashbacks?
5. Does the author use symbols or irony? Write down the recurrent symbols. Write down examples of irony, or at least note where they occur in the novel.
6. What is the setting of the novel? Where are the characters, what are they doing? Is the setting important to the story? Does the setting provide a framework for the story?
7. What is the theme of the novel? Can you write down in

one sentence what message the author is trying to convey?

8. Does the author make any unusual use of language? Are the author's sentences short, simple, and direct; or are they long and full of subordinate clauses? Does the author use dialect? How effective is the author's style of sentences at conveying meaning?

WORKSHEET FOR A SHORT STORY

1. What is the title? As you read the title, does it bring to mind an image? Who is the author?
2. What is the setting and who are the characters? How well developed are the characterizations? Do the characters' names tell you anything about them?
3. What is the plot of the story? Everything depends on the story line; without knowing it, you will lose track of other things.
4. Does the author create any abrupt contrasts such as light-dark, hot-cold, or contrasts of character? Does the author use the contrast for dramatic effect or to convey extra meaning in brief form?
5. Does one of the characters tell the story? If so, how does that affect the story?

WORKSHEET FOR A PLAY

1. Who is the author? When and where did the author live?
2. Are there conventions of stagecraft particular to this author's era? How do these conventions limit what the author can do? Do the conventions affect the stage, scenery, actors, and characters?
3. What is the title? What does it tell you about the play?
4. What is the setting? What are the circumstances that have led up to the opening scene? (You probably will not be able to answer these questions until you have read the play.)
5. Is there a plot, is there action? Write down the story line briefly. (There may not be much action in some plays.)
6. Does the author use symbol, irony, metaphor, or other figures of speech? Are things as they appear on the surface, or is there deeper meaning underlying characters, actions, or scenes?
7. Can you classify the play as a tragedy or a comedy? How does the play fit into one or the other of these categories?

If it is neither a tragedy or a comedy, why does neither of these terms apply?

8. Can you write in a sentence what the play's theme is?

WORKSHEET FOR A POEM

1. Who is the author? When and where did the author live?
2. What is the title of the poem? Is it a fitting title? Does the title bring any image to mind?
3. Does the poem fit into a framework determined by rhyme and meter (for example, iambic pentameter) or determined by number of syllables (as in haiku)? Or is there no framework at all?
4. What does the poem tell you? Does it describe an emotion, a moment, or tell a story?
5. How does the author use language? Are there symbols, similes, metaphors? What images do the author's words convey? (Remember that poets try to convey their meaning in few words, and so even single words can convey great meaning.)

WORKSHEET FOR AN ESSAY

1. Who is the author? When and where did the author live?
2. What is the title of the essay? Is the title meaningful?
3. What is the author's thesis? What is the author arguing about or trying to prove?
4. Does the author use examples to illustrate the main points? What are some examples? Are the examples valid?
5. Does the author make an impassioned plea? How logical is the argument? Does the author make false assertions or denials?
6. Does the author argue successfully? Why is the author successful; or why does the author fail?

Composition

Often in English class you will be asked to write essays in response to the literature you are reading. As you write, you will be bringing into play what you know about grammar and literature; so, in a sense, composition is the culmination of your training in English.

For your essay writing to be forceful, you need to organize your thoughts carefully, present your arguments in a logical manner, and write sentences that are not only grammatical but also interesting to read. To organize your thoughts, create a brief outline, either on paper or in your mind, before writing; and as you create the outline, review the order of your ideas to check for errors in logical arrangement. To write sentences that are interesting to read, strive to pack several ideas into each sentence, and try to express repeated concepts in different words. Short, choppy sentences of one or two ideas and the use of the same words over and over again are the marks of an immature writer. Be on guard, however, against creating excessively long sentences; their very length may detract from their quality.

Below is a checklist to use after you have composed an essay, but before you turn the essay in for a grade.

CHECKLIST FOR COMPOSITION
1. Have you followed your teacher's instructions about format? (Name in correct place, proper kind of paper, proper color of ink, and so on.)
2. Is your spelling correct?
3. Is your punctuation correct?
4. Do most of your sentences contain several ideas? Beware of piling up masses of short, single-idea sentences; they can be boring.
5. Is there sufficient variety in your vocabulary? Beware of repetition of words. Beware also of using odd or archaic words merely for variety.
6. Check any sentence longer than thirty words. Is it a good sentence? Might it be better as two sentences? If you are satisfied with it, leave it alone, but do check it once!
7. Is every sentence grammatically correct?

History

History is the study of the past; the study of events, their causes and effects; the study of ideas, their origin and effects; and the study of people, and how they affected the world around them.

What is the purpose of all this study of the past? One sage wrote that men who do not know the past are forced to relive it, thus implying that history's purpose is to instruct the present. Sherman Kent has written, "knowledge of things said and done . . . not merely sees us through the trivial decisions of the moment, but also stands by in the far more important times of personal or public crisis."[1] Leopold Van Ranke, the great German historian of the nineteenth century who created the modern historical method, disclaims such a lofty educational purpose for history. He thought that history ought merely show what happened. Whatever the purpose history holds for you, it can be an exciting course of study.

The historical method will sharpen your skills in critical thinking. It will be your best training ground for becoming efficient in making sound judgments; for the historical method consists of those processes by which truth is separated from falsehood, fact is distinguished from opinion, effects are measured in the light of causes, and conditions and situations are weighed in relationship to probability and consequence.

In history class you will have to recognize what facts are, and be able to contrast them with statements of opinion. You will have to organize facts clearly to write essays; and you will have to assess your sources, judging whether they are eyewitness accounts (primary sources) or second-hand accounts (secondary sources). You also will have to determine the bias of your source and judge the validity of the information it contains.

To succeed as a student of history you will need to pay particular attention to facts, for without them you will be unable to support your arguments in your essays. Use the *who, where, when, what,* and *why* method for remembering details of your history lesson. Put the *person* in the *place* at the right *time,* know *what* he did and *why* he was there. The five *w*'s make a complete picture. They bring the parts of the puzzle together. For example: Leonidas, the heroic Spartan king (who) was at Ther-

---

1. Sherman Kent, *Writing History,* 2nd ed. (New York: Meredith Publishing Co., 1967), 1.

mopylae in northern Greece (where) in August 480 B.C. (when) leading a small force of Spartans and other Greeks (what) in a vain attempt to prevent (why) Xerxes' army from invading southern Greece. The five *w*'s also make an outline upon which the whole exciting, heroic story of Leonidas comes back to you detail by detail. If you will practice the *who, where, when, what,* and *why* method for remembering your history lesson, you will find that many details, once lost, will remain with you. The five *w*'s method of creating a complete picture of events is used by newspaper writers to present a clear story, and by lawyers to present clear and complete evidence to juries in court. Use it for studying your history lesson.

The author of your history book did not mean that you should repeat (parrot-like) his very words when you are answering questions in class. Practice using your own words when you review your lesson. Even in your first reading of the assignment, if you find yourself with a group of words that do not seem to make a passage clear to you, put it in your own words.

This will not only help you remember your history, but will help you to express clearly what you wish to say. And the ability to put your thoughts into clear expression, to communicate your ideas to others, is the ability which, more than any other, will make you a success or a failure in life.

The maps in your history book were put there for you to use. They show more clearly than any words can describe where you are going in your history. Maps, diagrams, graphs, genealogy charts, simple designs, and illustrations are important visual aids to help you. Remember, there is much truth in the old adage: "One picture is worth a thousand words." But don't forget to read the words under the picture; they were also put there to help you.

Diagrams may show what happens to surplus food produced by American farmers; they may show how the population of Egypt was arranged by social classes; they may show names and duties of the twelve chief deities of the Greek Pantheon (pan— union, theos—god; thus, union or group of gods). Such diagrams may be animated to such a degree as to bring the information completely alive. They can be used to fix in your mind a permanent picture.

Use diagrams to help you remember details; there is no better help. Practice making simple drawings of your own to visualize your lesson. After you have read how the stones were put into place on the Great Pyramid, draw a simple figure to illustrate the long earthen ramp up which the stones were moved. This is learning by doing, one of the best ways to learn.

Geography influences the whole life of a people. Geographical influences may range from the clearness of the skies over Greece to the number of goats roaming a mountainside. The sky with its incredible blueness reflected in the Mediterranean softened the harshness of the rugged mountain contours and gave the Greeks a perspective of beauty unequaled in the world. They set their white soft-lined temples against the blue skylines, a setting so natural that the temples seem to be a part of nature. Dreaming under their sunlit sky, they developed an art of living that is forever mirrored for the world in their cultural achievement.

Yet their daily existence was as severe as the hills and mountains around them. The goats that roamed the mountains ate the young tree sprouts. Forests to prevent erosion never had a chance to grow. The topsoil washed into the sea, and the Greeks forever struggled to coax a precarious living from the land; so much so that a Spartan king once remarked: "Poverty is our companion from childhood." The same geographical influence sent the Greeks across the sea searching for better fields to cultivate; thus, they spread their civilization over the whole Mediterranean.

Geography has always influenced history. As you study history, make geography supply you with many answers for questions that ask "Why?"

Hints for Studying History

1. Keep a list of important names, dates, events, and ideas in your notebook at the front of the section of notes.

2. Use a study method, as discussed in Chapter 5. History is the academic discipline best suited to the use of study methods.

3. Use a worksheet for dealing with your textbook. Use the sample work sheet that follows, or adapt it to your own needs.

WORKSHEET FOR TEXTBOOK ASSIGNMENTS IN HISTORY
1. What do I know about this assignment?
2. What can I find out about this assignment from a quick scan of the boldface type?
3. What do the study questions at the end of the chapter tell me about the assignment?
4. How does this assignment relate to previous assignments?
5. Read the assignments and take notes, using the ⅓–⅔ format.
6. What topics of importance was I unable to predict in Part 2 and 3 above?
7. What are the important names, dates, in this assignment? *Remember* the five w's—*who, where, when, what, why.*
8. What questions will my teacher ask on tests about this assignment?

As part of your study of history, you may be asked to write research papers; and in doing the research for these, you will need to pay attention to the special demands the academic discipline of history places upon you. In addition to the regular requirements of research, you will need to weigh the validity of your sources. Primary sources are documents, letters, papers, speeches, and the like, that were written by people directly involved in the process or event you are investigating. These documents are eyewitness accounts, so to speak. Because they were written by people close to the origin of the event, these documents are to be considered of greater value than opinions written by men and women not directly involved. The letters, papers, speeches, or books written by men and women who did not take part in the event are called secondary sources.

If, for example, you were doing a research paper on the conflict between President Andrew Jackson and Nicholas Biddle over the United States Bank, primary sources would be letters, speeches, and notes by either man or by men who helped them during the conflict. Secondary sources would be such works as Marquis James's biography of Jackson, or Arthur Schlesinger, Jr.'s book, *The Age of Jackson.*

You may find it helpful to use worksheets in addition to your regular note-taking method when you are doing your research, so as to help you distinguish your primary sources from your secondary ones, and to weigh the importance of each source. Below are two worksheets.

WORKSHEET FOR PRIMARY SOURCES IN HISTORY

1. Who is the author of this document?
2. What do I know about the author?
3. When did the author write the document?
4. What sort of document is this? (Letter, speech, *etc.*)
5. For what purpose did the author write?
6. What can I expect to get out of this document?
7. What does this document say? (Write your notes according to the system you have already determined to use— on notecards, for example.)
8. Does this document meet my expectations, as I expressed them above in my answer to Question 6? If not, why not?
9. What topics does this document encourage me to study in other sources or texts?

WORKSHEET FOR SECONDARY SOURCES IN HISTORY

1. Who is the author of this work? When did the author write this work?
2. Does this author present a balanced argument, or is his argument heavily weighted in one direction? If weighted in one direction, in which one?
3. For what purpose am I reading this work?
4. Make notes, according to the system you already have determined to use—on note cards, for example.
5. What other secondary sources does this work suggest I read?
6. What primary sources does this work suggest I read?

Mathematics

Mathematics is basic to the development of our whole society. Without it, our technology would cease to exist, our economy grind to a halt, and all our scientific knowledge would cease to be usable. In everyday life, each one of us must use mathematics constantly, comparing prices, interest rates; determining when is the optimum time to purchase products, or to put money into savings accounts, or into some other form of investment; even in our pastimes we use mathematics, to calculate courses when sailing or to figure how much food to bring along on a picnic. In business, the need for mathematics is greater now than ever before; shop foremen must read complicated drawings, make minute measurements, and measure angles; salespeople must figure production costs and profit when bidding for a contract; managers of business must know how to use statistics, read graphs, and make calculations based on them. The list is endless.

Those of you who are bound for college will need to study mathematics carefully in order to prepare yourselves for further study in many academic disciplines. Indeed, almost every academic discipline now employs some mathematics. Without serious study of mathematics including probability, statistics, and calculus, you will be at a great disadvantage, and may even be excluded from advanced study in most academic disciplines outside the humanities. You may find yourselves cut off from economics, sociology, psychology, as well as the sciences and mathematics! Since mathematics is so necessary for modern life, study it thoroughly and for as many years as you can.

Underlying all study in mathematics, whether in arithmetic or in calculus, is the basic task of problem solving. Each division of mathematics requires its own processes, but in each, students read problems in their textbooks, are taught to solve problems in class, and are tested by being asked to solve problems.

There are several things you can do to enhance your performance in mathematics classes.

1. Take note of the format of the textbooks you use. These books may have visual aids to help you identify significant ideas: different colors of print, shaded areas, or boxes. Your textbooks also will have sample problems, with all the steps included, in order to show you the necessary steps in the correct process of reaching an answer. And, of course, there will be many problems for you to solve by using the procedures illustrated by the sample problems. In many recent textbooks there is an answer key at the back so that you may check your work for accuracy.

2. Pay close attention in class to what your teacher is saying and doing, and make careful notes. (Be sure to label your paper as class notes, and be sure to put the date at the top.) Copy down the problems your teacher solves on the board, since they will probably be problems containing the essence of the topic under discussion. (These problems may also be typical of problems you will find on quizzes and tests.) Do not take these class notes on your homework papers. If you do, you will confuse what you have done at home with what you have done in class, and there might be errors on your homework paper that will confuse you as you study from the notes later.

3. As soon as you can after mathematics class, rework the problems your teacher put on the board during class. If you cannot do these soon after class, at least make sure to rework them before beginning your homework. By solving these problems again, you will be reinforcing all the knowledge you have gained from that day's class.

4. Try to be as neat as you can when taking notes in class, when completing assignments, and when taking tests. Write your symbols clearly and large enough to be read easily, and make sure that the problems are clearly separated from one another on the page. Also, try to be complete, showing the work you have done to reach the answer. Finally, when you are doing homework,

leave space for your corrections, so that if your solution is wrong, you can correct the error on the page.

5. Read your text carefully; read with paper and pencil in hand; and as you read, notice the visual aids in the text and what they are highlighting. When you come across a sample problem, cover the solution with paper and solve the problem yourself. Then check your solution with the one in the text to make sure that you have the correct answer and that you have included all the proper steps.

6. Do all homework assignments only after reading your text, solving the sample problems correctly, and reviewing your notes from class. After you have solved an assigned problem, compare your answer with the one in the answer key at the back of the textbook. If your answer is incorrect, solve the problem again, and compare your answer again. If you still are incorrect, put a star beside the problem on your homework paper, and ask your teacher about that problem at the start of your next class.

7. Perhaps most important of all, keep all old quizzes and tests. Quizzes will show what your teacher thinks is important and will identify typical problems. Use these quizzes as guides for studying for tests, and solve the problems on them again as part of your studying for tests. Because tests on a chapter of the textbook will identify problems of major significance, you will benefit if you use them as study guides for unit tests and exams. As with quizzes, solve the problems again as part of your studying.

8. Finally, learn to use all the electronic aids available to you. Learn to use calculators and computers. These machines can do many of the computations you will do in mathematics classes and for homework at incredible speed. They are marvelous tools, but beware, they cannot do the learning for you. Remember that these machines are merely tools, you still will need to master the concepts and processes of mathematics.

Science

The sciences you are most likely to study in school are general science or physical science, biology, chemistry, and physics. Common to all these scientific studies is a method of inquiry, usually called the scientific method. The scientific method has three basic parts: the collection of data, the creation of hypotheses, and the experimentation to test the validity of the hypotheses. These parts need not come in the order given, but for any scientific inquiry to be complete, the scientist must perform all three parts. In science classes in school you generally will be given a statement of fact or a hypothesis and will be asked to collect information and conduct an experiment to validate the statement or hypothesis.

Scientists generally use the metric system of measurement rather than the American or English system. Below is a chart of equivalents to guide you as you make conversions.

1 inch = 2.54 centimeters	1 centimeter = 0.3937 inch
1 foot = 0.3048 meter	1 meter = 3.2808 feet
1 yard = 0.9144 meter	1 meter = 1.0936 yards
1 mile = 1.6093 kilometers	1 kilometer = 0.6241 mile
1 quart = 0.9464 liter	1 liter = 1.0567 quarts
1 gallon = 3.7854 liters	1 liter = 0.2642 gallon
1 ounce = 28.3495 grams	1 gram = 0.0353 ounce
1 pound = 0.4536 kilogram	1 kilogram = 2.2046 pounds

There are some things you can do in science class to improve the quality of your studying, things that are useful in any of the sciences.

1. Make a quick survey of the chapters of your textbook. Is there a preliminary paragraph in the chapters that tells you what you will be learning? Are important terms printed in boldface type or in italics? Are units of the chapters numbered? Are there study questions at the end of the chapters, or perhaps summaries or review

outlines? Are there visual aids to help signal important information (such things as boxes, shaded areas, different colors of print)?

2. Look at the back of the textbook for a glossary and an index. The glossary will be helpful when you are learning new technical terms, the index will help you find a topic easily when you are reviewing. Check also for appendices. Many textbooks have several kinds of charts, lists of important scientific laws, formulas, and other types of important information in sections at the back of the book. Check also for an answer key if your textbook contains problems to solve. You will be able to check your answers for accuracy if there is an answer key.

3. Make sure to follow all instructions carefully when you are doing laboratory work. Take careful notes in a laboratory notebook, and make sure not to mingle your lab notes with the notes you take in class or from your textbook. Make sure to write clearly in your lab notebook and to take down all the necessary information. Illegible notes and incomplete lab notes will prevent you from having the information necessary to complete your report of the experiment.

There are also some things to do when preparing for science class that are fairly specific to the science being studied.

General Science or Physical Science

Follow all procedures carefully, since it is likely that in a general science course you will be introduced to laboratory work for the first time. Also, pay close attention to the scientific method, and make sure that you understand it and how to perform all three functions.

Biology

1. Learn how biological scientists have classified information about living things and what is the reasoning

process that is the basis for the classification system. You may be required to memorize some of this system, and your understanding of how the system works will make this task easier.

2. In a special section of your notebook, make a list of the biological terms you need to know. This list may become very long and may be a very important part of your notebook, for important terms in biology are perhaps more numerous than in other sciences.

3. Pay close attention to the details of the drawings that your teacher puts on the board and that are in your textbook. Make sure that the drawings you put in your notes are both accurate and clear.

Chemistry

1. Recognize that it is very important to know and to understand the procedures to be used in chemistry. Learn *why* you are following a certain procedure, since merely memorizing the steps in a procedure will not usually give you sufficient knowledge to adapt it to new situations or experiments.

2. Most of the work you do in problem solving in the first year of your study of chemistry will call upon an understanding of many of the procedures you learned in algebra. Be ready to apply what you have learned in algebra to your problem solving in chemistry. If you haven't studied algebra already when you begin chemistry, take heart, you will be able to keep up in class if you work hard to understand and apply the procedures used in problem solving as they are explained in your textbook or by your teacher. Also, many chemistry textbooks contain an appendix devoted to the mathematics necessary in chemistry. If you need extra help with the mathematics, look for such an appendix.

3. When reading your textbook, have paper and pencil in hand so that you can take notes and work out the equations given in the text.

Physics

1. As in chemistry, in physics it is necessary for you to understand why you are using procedures and performing operations. Mere memorization of steps will usually not be sufficient.

2. Also as in chemistry, in the first year of physics you will be able to use the knowledge you have gained of algebra. Be ready to transfer your learning to a new subject.

3. In class write the problems your teacher puts on the board clearly in your notebook, making sure to label them as class notes. It is likely these problems will be similar to the problems you will see on tests.

4. As you read your assignments, do so with paper and pencil, and practice working out problems and equations. As much as you can, practice solving problems and working out equations. Such efforts are never wasted.

A Final Word

This quick survey can do no more than scratch the surface of the nature and methodology of the different courses of study. You will have to be alert in class and careful in reading in order to pick up the specific information you will need to earn good grades. In general, although the courses do differ significantly, if you memorize specific information, learn the rules of method that govern the course, and apply both as you learn, you will do well.

Looking Back

1. While this chapter has different approaches for helping you to study more effectively in the major subject areas,

there are some suggestions that are common to all subjects. List three of them.

2. One of Oxford University's best known professors was retiring, and he invited several of his students to tea. They asked him to leave them with some words of advice. The old teacher replied, "I can sum up what is most important to all scholars in three words—*verify your sources!*"

    What was his meaning?

3. The first part of the scientific method is the collection of data. What are the other two parts?

9

A FEELING FOR SCHOOL SUBJECTS: IT GROWS FROM INTEREST

"Feeling is the golden ingredient that turns knowledge into wisdom."

True Confessions

1. Have you ever been asked by an adult, "What did you do in school today?" and answered, "Nothing."?

   Since it is obvious that you had done something, why did you answer that way? What makes a student bored with school? What would you think of young people who say that they are never truly bored in school?

2. Here are the programs of two juniors in the same high school. What conclusions, if any, can you draw about these students?

1.	Trigonometry
2.	Physics
3.	French III
4.	Computer Science
5.	Lunch
6.	American History
7.	English
8.	Gym

1.	English
2.	Math Fundamentals
3.	Gym
4.	Driver's Education
5.	Lunch
6.	Wood Shop
7.	Merchandising
8.	Study

How do these programs compare with yours?

3. What language, other than English, do you speak? Was it learned in the home or at school? It has been said that Americans are generally deficient in foreign language study. From your experience, is that true? If so, how can you explain it?

The Beginning of Success is Interest

What is learned should never be passively or mechanically received, as dead information which weighs down and dulls the mind. It must rather be actively transformed by understanding into the very life of the mind, and thus strengthen the latter, as wood thrown into fire and transformed into flame makes the fire stronger.[1]

It is the responsibility of the student to be interested. No one can be interested for you, and no one can increase your interest unless you so will. It is the basic obligation that you must take to class; it is the basic obligation that you must hold up to each assignment. In life it is the basic obligation you will carry into your life's work, or life will make you a person of no consequence or influence, going from job to job, thinking always that

1. Jacques Maritain, *Education at the Crossroads* (New Haven: Yale University Press, 1943), 50.

the grass will be greener on the other side of the fence, bored with things as they are because you were never interested enough to learn that it is only through ignorance that we are ever bored.

Do not expect that all assignments or even all subjects will hold a natural interest for you. Mathematics may seem unrewarding or English boring, while history is much more meaningful to you. If mathematics is the subject you like least, have the courage to do that assignment first. Mastering a subject that does not appeal to you will give you confidence in your ability to do difficult things as you go through life. Life is full of little duties that carry no immediate appeal, but the person who can tackle a job whether he likes it or not is the successful and happy one.

The effort of the will cannot be reduced to a simple formula or practice; interest cannot be learned as one learns a vocabulary or a law of science. Interest can be acquired best, perhaps, by starting with a determination that *there is scarcely any limit to what a human being can do if he is sufficiently interested.* And if one is sufficiently interested, the burdensome drudgery of study and work disappear. Then comes appreciation and feeling.

Try Interest Instead of Prejudice for Languages

The languages here referred to are those other than your native language, that being English for most of us. The word "foreign" carries a remote and alien connotation that can scarcely be called real in the world in which we live—since we are only a few hours away from people speaking Spanish, French, German, and Italian. And there was never very much that was foreign and remote about the classical languages, Latin and Greek. Every day we rely on them for supplying us with terms to name many of the things we use and for root words that make the very foundation of our own language. So, if you can avoid the use of the word "foreign," you will probably be taking the first step toward getting rid of a prejudice against studying languages other than your own.

Further aid in getting rid of a prevalent prejudice against other languages is to change your point of view. It is not totally accurate, as you sometimes feel, that you are forced to study another language for the accumulation of credits. Successful study of another language can be of great economic value. Imagine yourself in a position to be sent by your company or employer to a project or plant in another country. It happens all the time, and the lucky people to get the opportunity are those who have the language qualifications.

Speech, man's greatest invention, is the thing that makes us what we call "human" rather than "animal," providing a memory for mankind—the basis of all culture and civilization. This heritage is just as significant in Hebrew, Greek, Latin, French, German, Italian, and Spanish as it is in English. You can, therefore, approach the study of another language from the point of view that it makes possible one of the most broadening and cultural elements of your education.

The new set of speech habits comprising a new language will be learned to a very large degree the way you learned the language you use daily. You learned English by starting with a few words, actually with a few sounds. You did not forget them after you had used them one day, as if they were part of an assigned vocabulary for Thursday. You used these sounds over and over again—practice and more practice. In time, you could think in terms of the words you knew without saying them aloud. Your parents were happy because they didn't have to listen to you practice saying the word *dog* dozens of times each day. This, of course, seems very juvenile, but if you learn a new language, "a new set of speech rules," practice, practice, and more practice is going to be a very important part of the program.

You will learn the order in which these new words are arranged to make sense from the rules of grammar and the structure of the language. You may learn to read some of the language, and to speak it, before you learn the technical elements of construction. You certainly did this with your English. But an important factor in studying a language is to reconcile yourself to the importance of knowing the fundamentals of grammar. Perhaps a good way to start would be with an honest admission that, having missed learning many of the grammatical terms in studying English, a little study of English grammar would save you from immediate deficiencies.

A second immediate necessity in the study of another language is keeping up with each assignment. In no subject is the importance of rigid adherence to a schedule of day-to-day preparation as vital. Granted, it is neither advisable nor wise to get behind in a day's work in any class, but falling behind in vocabulary, reading assignments, idioms, and grammar in the study of another language is fatal.

Learning a language is to progress from one step to the next, and each requires mastery of the one preceding it. The steps are four in number. (1) You must learn the meaning of words before you can use them. (2) You must learn something about word order and idioms before you can use them to express an idea. (3) You must learn the various forms a word can take before you can use it in the right person, case, number, etc. (4) You must learn to pronounce the word in order to express what you have learned in the preceding steps.

There is a fifth step that few secondary school language students attain, but it should be your aim, for to accomplish it is to save half the time spent in reading and writing language assignments. This final step is to learn to think in the language. To think in the language means that when you see the Latin, French, or Spanish word for dog, you do not translate it into English, but use it as you find it—*canis* (Latin), *chien* (French), and *perro* (Spanish). Accomplishing this, you are prepared to use another language the way you use English. You do not turn English words into other words before you use them—doubling the time necessary to produce a thought picture. Practice learning to think in the language you are studying. Start simply; first, pick out familiar objects, and try to name them in the language directly, without first thinking of the English name; next, advance to simple thoughts about the object—the dog ran, the dog is gentle. This practice can lead to more complex thinking and mastery.

Try Smiles for Mathematics Instead of Frowns

Why does a child smile and excitedly wave its paper and pencil when it has suddenly discovered that $2 + 2 = 4$ and that 2×2 also equals 4? As with the child, this was once a great discovery by some ancient thinker who smiled because he knew his accomplishment was very great, and at the same time very puzzling. For he immediately tried it with the number three and it didn't work.

Ancient peoples' fascination and feeling for numbers have come down to us. Some ancient counted on his hairy fingers and discovered ten. In a place called Sumer, on the Euphrates River, about five thousand years ago, a people we call Sumerians made ten important. And today our decimal system is based on that important ten.

These same Sumerians also left us other number legacies. The excitement and feeling for numbers reached up into the heavens. They discovered that the moon changed its nature in seven days, and completely changed in four sevens. So they added up the four sevens and made a moon (lunar) month to measure time.

Both seven and four became special and favorite numbers, and spread far and wide. The biblical writers never tired of using them and their multiples of ten: "the seventh day," "seventy times seven," "seven days in a week," "four weeks in a month," "forty years in the wilderness," "forty-day journey."

The pages of history make it very clear that feeling for mathematics has never slackened once numbers were discovered. The ancient Egyptian used his forty-inch measuring reed (canon) to lay out the Great Pyramid, which covers thirteen acres. The ancient Babylonian measured and laid out his irrigation ditches and discovered a whole new field of mathematics; the part we call geometry—measuring geography measurements. So, this is mathematics: simple and mystic, practical and romantic, measuring the height of a child in inches and the distance to a star in light years—one about twenty-one inches, the other 5,880 billion miles.

Mathematics can serve you and can serve you profitably and with much pleasure, rather than you serving it as a resentful slave, waiting to finish the last required course so you will be free forever. And in this last thought you are surely mistaken. You will not be free unless you have an appreciation of the concepts of mathematics. You will not lose your interest in the world around you and the universe beyond you; and freedom to enjoy much of both depends upon a basic knowledge of mathematics, and how it has been used by others to unveil the secrets of earth and sky.

Where can we start to make the study of mathematics not unlike the study of your other subjects? Perhaps the basic step, as with all subjects, is to develop an interest in the intrinsic value of mathematics in your own experience, and in its importance to our whole education, society, and, indeed, our very existence.

To appreciate the value of mathematics, it is best to approach it as a way of looking at things. The poet sees the world in one light, the mathematician in another, but there is more than a modicum of truth in Klaus Weierstrass' statement that "No mathematician can be a complete mathematician unless he is also something of a poet." It, therefore, follows that if you enjoy looking at things in your literature class through the eyes of the poet, you are capable of enjoying looking at things as seen through the eyes of the mathematician.

The practical aspects of a mathematical outlook are too obvious and numerous to detain us here. From checking the numerical grade on a paper to determining the returns of your investment at 12 percent, from estimating how many miles your car goes on a gallon of gas to estimating whether or not sheep can be profitably raised in New England—for all these, and a score of other problems to be solved daily, we turn to mathematics.

In addition to making the world around you more interesting, and providing an indispensable part of your operative daily existence, mathematics as a specific school subject can serve you in the following ways.

1. It can improve your ability to think clearly and with precision. For although there is a great deal of memorize-recall-apply procedure in the study of mathematics, it lends itself to a plus quantity of creative thinking—applying old patterns to new things, often using the "hunch" or "guess" (the most creative thing of all) to find a new principle or relationship that was not anticipated in the question presented by the problem.

2. One of the most significant and practical benefits that can come from the study of mathematics is the improvement of one's powers of observation. No reading requires keener observation of exactly what is written and precisely what is being asked. Powers of observation sufficient to visualize a condition or pattern are also necessary for the solving of problems. A man whose lot was one hundred fifty feet wide and who wished to build a fence across it with a post every ten feet went to the hardware store and bought fifteen posts. In school he had apparently not let his mathematics courses serve to improve his powers of observation. When he had installed his fifteen posts, he had to make another trip to the store.

3. The study of mathematics, accompanied by its history, can provide confidence in and respect and appreciation for the marvelous workings of the mind of man. Perhaps the most important single means of clearing away some of the stumbling blocks of attitude would be to go back and search out the fascinating history of how men invented numbers to count by—first on fingers, thus our decimal system of ten; then using many more by dou-

bling tens. We could learn how the Babylonians kept their records; or how Eratosthenes, with a deep well in Syene, Upper Egypt, and a posthole at Alexandria, a distance of 574 miles and an angle of 7° 12′, calculated the circumference of the earth to be 24,662 miles— missing by only 195 miles, or less than one percent. Or we could study Euclid, whose geometry takes second place only to the Bible in terms of the period of time it has remained in use, or Pythagoras and his theory, which the Babylonians probably knew long before him, or Archimedes, perhaps one of the half-dozen greatest brain machines who ever lived. We read the lives of poets and statesmen to appreciate their works. The same can be done with much pleasure in the march of mathematics and the men who have made it.

But our feeling for arithmetic or algebra or geometry cannot long survive based on the romantic and exciting discoveries and developments found in history. A practical approach is also necessary. This must include a determination to study our own skills and an understanding of the language of mathematics.

There are tests available in the basic skills—the handling of fractions, the use of equations, and the solution of simple word problems—which can be used to indicate areas where mistakes occur most frequently. Such a test is the sample Scholastic Aptitude Test that can be had at your school. Your teacher may be able to prepare a test for you. Perhaps weaknesses could be determined by a tabulation of types of mistakes made on homework papers. Once the trouble areas have been discovered, the same sensible steps of checking, awareness, and neatness that are applied to produce satisfactory results in other subjects will reap a like harvest in mathematics.

Proper outlook, positive thinking, and correcting obvious weaknesses bring you to the starting point for a pleasant and profitable experience in continuing your study of mathematics. The suggestions that follow can make this everything one could hope for as a fruitful learning experience.

A real feeling for mathematics will never be real without a real understanding of words and definitions. Although the scope of mathematics has increased more in the past three decades than it did in twenty-two centuries from Euclid to Einstein, the vocabulary of mathematics has grown even faster. As a matter of fact, mathematics has almost a dual vocabulary—the old and the new. The so-called "New Mathematics" gives new and broader meaning to old patterns and concepts through a *new* vocabulary. The old words—addition and multiplication—are still in use, but new words—arrays, sets, group, field, and a whole covey of words ending in morphism (meaning form)—are now found in your math book. You will need to use the definition of the particular book you are studying; so the index should be used as a guide to review basic words until you know them. Reference has been made to the importance of a basic vocabulary list for each subject, arranged in a notebook for handy use.

Studying Science

Your own science course in school—whether general science, biology, chemistry, or physics—can deepen your appreciation of the world in which you live and add new dimensions to that world. The study of science will demand an exactness in reasoning, a precision in observation, and a thoroughness in execution similar to those required of you in mathematics; for, of course, mathematics is the beginning of science.

The study methods applied to a general textbook reading assignment will also apply to science: (1) the preliminary survey with its accompanying question, What am I supposed to learn from this assignment? (2) the selective reading (intensive for all rules, theories, and formulas), the careful reading of illustrative material, and the reading to be accompanied by a thorough study of all graphic material (diagrams, charts, etc.); (3) the reciting of material to yourself by scanning topics and signals such as boldface, italics, and enumerations; (4) the review of those sections that do not come immediately to mind.

The principles of order, precision, and thoroughness required in the execution of the written work of mathematics should be applied with equal care to science papers. For some written work in sciences like biology, a little painstaking artistic work (such as contrasting colors) can add much to show your teacher that you have the indispensable element for excellence—a sense of pride in your work.

Fundamental to a feeling for science is the master list of several important parts of the particular course, be it general science, biology, chemistry, or physics. All students should keep, from the first day of the course, a master list of technical and specialized words and terms that constitute the scientific vocabulary of the course. Some of these words are new and difficult to spell. The application of language sense and relationship can help greatly in this respect, for many of them, or their roots, have been seen in Latin or French. Some science students find review easier if the master list is put on cards rather than in a science notebook.

The second master list should contain theories and laws that recur with such frequency as to be primary to understanding cumulative cases and problems. These should be stated as briefly as possible, and the page number of the text where they are described in full should be written beside each.

The third master list should contain the distinctive formulas, equations, devices, and properties essential to working out the concepts or principles of the subject. This master list will be quite different in size from one science subject to another, and for the sake of workability, should be kept to a minimum.

The master lists provide the basic working material of the science course. Having learned these, the mastery of the subject is largely applying what is known to arrive at the solution (the unknown). It is in a very real sense vocabulary ability—that is, deriving patterns and practical solutions from numerical and linguistic forms of language that have been given. If you can think of your science course in this light, it will become much easier, and understanding and a feeling of appreciation will replace frustration.

"I just like the feel of the tools in my hands" is a statement heard from many a master craftsman. Some science courses make this possible. There is much in the content of all science subjects that lends itself to demonstration by models. With a supply of wire and soft wood blocks, some cardboard, and a box of colored pencils, you are provided with the material for the most effective of all learning processes—learning by doing.

In the realm of learning by doing, the *diagram*, the *sketch*, the *illustration*, the *graph*, and the *table* can also be of great value in understanding the text and operating with a degree of excellence in the laboratory. Since the study of science demands exactness, each of the figures named above is designed to perform a specific function.

A diagram shows relationships. It deals mainly with how one factor affects another as changes are introduced. Diagrams have, perhaps, their greatest use in showing cycles, such as the cycle of oxygen or carbon, or the action of sunlight on chlorophyll to form carbohydrates in living plants from water and carbon dioxide (photosynthesis). Diagrams may also be used in series very effectively to show phases or steps in logical sequence.

The sketch is designed to make clear by reasonable reproduction. It is a teaching and learning device that is older than speech. It is useful in cutting down the quantity of class notes, is excellent for showing how parts interact; and as an aid to learning, fulfills the old adage that "a picture is worth a thousand words." The sketch must, of course, reflect a background of study showing that you understand the nature of the object. To this should be added a sense of proportion, neatness, and your full ability as a painstaking and careful artist. The illustration evolves from the sketch and presents as nearly a perfect reproduction as possible—the difference between sketch and illustration lies in the respective words used to define them, *reasonable* and *perfect* (perhaps *faithful* would be a more sensible word than *perfect*).

The graph, closely related to the diagram in form, performs the function of comparing two or more things by enumerative or graphic measurement, whereas the diagram shows interplay or effect of one factor upon another. The table, which is used in all science subjects, is a convenient and graphic way of listing much information and also of showing relationships. In addition to the many tables found in your science textbooks, you can use tables to show progression of events, growth, items, and functions.

In science study, work done in the laboratory is essential to understanding and application. Laboratory activity centers upon learning by doing. It is designed to provide concrete observation, investigation, and discovery. The student who thinks in terms of a scientific career should use the laboratory for developing technical skills in dealing with equipment as well as learning the subject matter of the course through experimentation.

Remembering the five steps in reasoning and applying them to the study of science is in reality what "the scientific method" of procedure requires. Its five steps proceed from the following: (1) gathering data, (2) classifying and organizing data, (3) generalizing to get principles and theories, (4) verifying generalizations by experiments, and (5) subjecting results to verification and proof.

To all the good study methods—rules of neatness, exactness, and thoroughness—background knowledge can add incentive and interest to make the study of science more meaningful. Above all else, perhaps the most profound and lasting feeling for science can come from reading biographies of the people who pursued ideas and dreams, and experiments and proofs, until they stretched the world in an atom, a cell, a life span, a universe.

History—Enjoy What You Cannot Avoid

The interpretation that one makes of history determines to a large degree the direction of one's life. No one can escape history, and no one can avoid interpretation.

Frequently, the student who does poorly in history will try to defend lack of interest by some such silly statement as "I am not interested in what is past, I am only interested in the present." If this sadly misdirected person could, by his own wishes, rid himself of history, he would "in the twinkling of an eye" reduce himself to the basic survival instinct and intellectual level of the lower animals.

Let us, using a case that seems within the realm of possibility, rid our person who has no interest in history from his contact with the past. Scientists are able to produce a gas capable of producing mass amnesia over a whole battlefront or city. Suppose enough of such a gas could be let loose to drift over the whole earth, following the prevailing winds over land and sea. Over the whole earth, progressively as the wind moved, history would be erased. The memory of the past, the total past, would be gone in an instant. The whole of mankind would be plunged abruptly into savagery. A person reading a book would stare blankly. Our friend who had no interest in the past, halfway home from school, would wander aimlessly, not remembering where he lived. He could meet others wandering with blank expressions, even his own parents, and neither would recognize the other. The point of the story is plain; if the past has no meaning, the present has no meaning, and there is no future.

So history for each of us is concerned with human knowledge and human need; and from the time when men first began to record the stories of men and things, they seem to have been gifted with a quality of mystic wisdom whereby they preordained or predetermined the goodness and necessity of their story for all who would come after them. The unknown biographer who wrote the deathless life of David in the *Old Testament* did not know that he was stamping "the great man, the great person" as the miracle of history. Herodotus, as has been written of him, "probably never asked himself what history was good for," but he found it a good and wonderful quality of entertainment. Thucydides found in history a deeper and more useful good—lessons for the future from the incidents of the past. The patterns of the good of history have continued down through the centuries.

Each generation rewrites the history of the world in the light of new problems facing it, and its concern is ever with the human knowledge and the human necessity of each individual who comprises its generation.

Students frequently fail to get the most possible from history because they view it somewhat after the manner of the five blind men feeling the elephant. The results are an awareness of parts only—names, dates, events without relationships, and places without geographical or cultural implications; seeing, as it were, the trees without the forest. The true perspective of history is not the view through a microscope, and even a telescopic lens will not be sufficient. One needs to look at history from a cycloramic point of view, supplemented by sufficient reflective power to mirror the observer himself; for only by seeing one's self as a part of the whole story of universal history, can meaning become clear and meaningful. It is commendable to know the date when Lincoln was born, and the exact moment when his heart stopped on that fateful April morning in 1865. But it is far more important to understand, or at least to ponder, why men of earth rise up and destroy the great among them. It is far more important for the history student to ask himself what part he has played in the assassinations before and after Lincoln. For if it is people who make people as they are—what have we made in our making?

Only when you have learned to think historically can you put yourself into history. Everyday experiences teach us that to get the most out of something, we must take an active part and become completely involved, to the extent that we feel that we are a part and "belong." Belonging leads to a feeling of relationship. Relationship historically leads us to an appreciation of something larger than ourselves. Almost every human being believes that there is a great intelligence, or cause, or guiding force, back of all our existence. Thinking historically helps us become more aware of a relationship that makes it possible for us to be more stable, to be more capable of accepting conditions beyond our immediate control, to seem more worthwhile to the world around us, and to find better reasons for our existence.

English Gives Meaning to Feeling

We need say little here. We have saturated this book with the importance of words and how necessary it is for you to learn to handle them correctly and wisely.

If you missed the examples we have given of how words, and the beauty and power that can be coaxed from them, have made possible the achievement and influence of Abraham Lincoln and Winston Churchill, you will miss a chance to see how important all your English courses are. If a course requires that a sentence be written, make it a best sentence. If it is a course that requires reading a novel or a poem, use your head, but give your heart a chance—this is the meaning of feeling:

> To follow knowledge like a
> sinking star
> Beyond the utmost bounds of
> human thought.[2]

It was a wise man named Blaise Pascal who said, "The heart has its reasons. . . ."

Looking Back

1. In language study, "the importance of rigid adherence to a schedule of day-to-day preparation" is vital. Why do you think we made such a strong statement in this chapter? Tell why you agree or disagree with our position.

2. Let us assume that you have been asked to tutor the

---

2. Alfred Lord Tennyson, *Collected Poems* (London: Macmillan Co., 1842), 72.

weakest biology student in your class. What plan might you develop in order to help that classmate?

3. What did the quotation, "No mathematician can be a complete mathematician unless he is also something of a poet" mean to you? What possible relationship is there between those two areas?

10

READING: FASTER WITH MORE UNDERSTANDING

True Confessions

1. I'm a fast reader, all right," Stewart said. "The only trouble is that I can't remember what I read."

    Is Stewart's problem your problem? Have you ever "read" an entire page or chapter in a book without being able to remember any of the material you just covered? Is there an easy cure for this common experience?

2. Ellis said, "I can generally remember names because of my system of connections. For example, when I'm introduced to someone named Harry Butler, I think of a hairy servant. Rose Graves was easy—a red flower on a tombstone. But I'm having difficulty with Feodor Dostoyevsky!"

    What system, if any, do you use to remember names?

3. Generally, we read different material in different ways. For example, you might approach your chemistry book with more determination than you would use on a Dick Tracy comic book.

Is there any difference in the way you concentrate on the following?

poetry	gossip column
sports pages	directions for repairing a TV set
book for a class report	romantic paperback

The Nature of Reading

"Reading is to the mind what exercise is to the body," was said by the English essayist Joseph Addison, in 1711 and echoed by designer Calvin Klein in his TV commercials in 1981. Unless we enrich our own thoughts by the great legacy of thought put in books for us, our minds miss the exercise needed for development, and perform with no greater measure of efficiency than the athlete who has neither trained nor practiced. As knowledge of words improves reading, so reading improves knowledge of words; for words are the tools of thinking, and reading is the storehouse from which comes most of our thinking.

The three objectives of a good reader are: (1) to concentrate on what is being read, (2) to remember as much as possible, (3) to apply or associate what is read to one's own experience. The three general types of reading are: (1) *Skimming*—this is quick scanning to find a particular fact (when Alexander the Great died or what follows Lincoln's "with malice toward none" phrase). Skimming may also be rapid reading for the main idea without bothering to gather accompanying details. (2) *Careful Reading*—this is reading that directs itself toward finding the main topics, fixing them in mind, judging what the important details are, and relating them to the main topics. (3) *Intensive Reading*—this is reading that directs itself to mastery of technical material, instructions in textbooks and on tests, textbook information that is cumulative, these requiring intensive reading that demands total understanding.

These types refer chiefly to work-type reading rather than reading for pleasure, although it is questionable whether anyone having a desire to learn does not always read with a great degree of pleasure. All practices for the development of better reading habits deal in one way or another with three aspects: (1) what to look for, (2) how to improve comprehension, (3) how to increase speed. As in methods of studying an assignment, it soon becomes apparent that different practices for improvement are generally variations rather than separate approaches. After you have seen the suggestions for improving the three areas noted above, you will then choose and modify according to your individual needs. Perhaps you can make new methods that will serve you better. If you are like the great majority of readers, your first and most difficult task will be to convince yourself that you can improve your reading habits. The almost universal attitude is that after the formal reading instruction of the first four or five years of elementary school, we *know how to read*—and with these final words the judgment is definite and further investigation unnecessary.

The pages of literature are filled with testimony that bears witness to the diligence in both practice and time if one is to constantly improve his reading ability. Listen to Johann Wolfgang von Goethe, poet, novelist, and philosopher, "The dear good people don't know how long it takes to learn to read. I've been at it eighty years, and can't say yet that I've reached the goal."

Henry David Thoreau, in his classic, *Walden, or Life in the Woods*, includes an essay on reading. Indeed, the whole of *Walden*, available in several paperback editions, would be an excellent practice field for the three areas of improvement. Thoreau says of reading (the italics are the author's):

> To read well—that is, to read true books in a true spirit—is a *noble exercise*, and one that will *task the reader more than any exercise* which the customs of the day esteem. *It requires* a *training* such as the *athletes underwent*, the *steady intention almost* of the *whole life* to this object. *Books must be read as deliberately and reservedly as they were written.*[1]

---

1.   Henry David Thoreau, *Walden*, or *Life in the Woods* (New York: The Heritage Press, 1939), 110.

Continuing in the same essay, he writes:

The works of the great poets have never yet been read by mankind, for only great poets can read them. They have only been read as the multitude read the stars, at most astrologically, not astronomically. Most men have learned to read to serve a paltry convenience, as they have learned to cipher (count) in order to keep accounts and not be cheated in trade; but *of reading as a noble intellectual exercise they know little or nothing, yet this only is reading in a high sense*, not that which lulls as a luxury and suffers the nobler faculties to sleep the while, but *what we have to stand* on top-toe to read and *devote* our *most alert* and *wakeful* hours to.[2]

What to Look For

The first practice for the improvement of reading ability is to know what to look for. You must look for ideas. How can you train yourself to look for ideas and thoughts rather than at words? Words are merely the symbols and labels used to portray the thoughts of the author. The reader does not take the words from the printed page; they remain. What the reader takes from the page are ideas and thoughts (idea is used here to designate a portion of a thought); consequently, they are what the reader must train himself to find. Mere word reading hinders this process of finding ideas. Perhaps the best way to rid one's self of word-reading is to begin all reading by getting a quick bird's-eye-view.

Turn back to the quotations from Thoreau. Do not plod from word to word. Skim rapidly over the passages and try to pick up from the italicized sections the main thought: Reading is a noble intellectual exercise, requiring more training than most people are willing to devote to it. Now go back and enjoy reading the entire passage. The facts will not become jumbled and confusing, and the organization and purpose will stand out clearly.

Since it is plain that the best way to obtain a bird's-eye-view is to find quickly the core of the paragraph, then each paragraph

2. Ibid., 110.

indentation should alert the reader. The quick motion of going over the paragraph for the central thought removes the stagnant, almost motionless operation of the word-reader, creeping up on a word, or as it sometimes seems, waiting for the word to crawl to the reader. A second result of this practice is to give the reader an awareness of thoughts. This may be compared to looking at the forest first and then approaching to look at the trees. The return to pick out the contributing ideas from the sentences that make up the paragraph is comparable to looking at the trees, but no one looks at every tree in the forest—only significant ones are observed. Perhaps this procedure could be best remembered by the formula:

$$P + S = CT$$
Paragraph + Sentence = Complete Thought

A formula for what to look for in reading without a *W* to stand for *words*—how strange! You will, of course, see words, but only as necessary labels for ideas. They will no longer be the purpose for which you are reading.

Knowing what to look for in reading presupposes a basic knowledge of paragraph patterns and sentence structure. What a paragraph is, quick recognition of how it is developed, ability to focus in on the topic sentence, getting the idea label from sentences—these are the things the reader must look for and see instantly. The four basic types of paragraphs are *exposition, description, narration,* and *argumentation.* These basic forms of discourse may be put in various patterns of paragraphs: (1) question and answer, (2) comparison and contrast, (3) cause and effect, (4) opinion and proof, (5) repetition of example, and (6) multiplication of details. Models are available in your English handbook. One or two examples will show you how quickly comprehension follows if you know exactly what you are looking for.

Here is a question and answer paragraph (the italics are the author's):

How should you read? As you please. If you please yourself by reading fast, read fast; if you read slowly and do not feel like reading faster, read slowly. Pascal does not say we are apt to read too fast or too slowly, but he blames only an excess. Montaigne complains of a formal way of reading. "My thoughts go to sleep when they are seated," he says, "so they and I walk." Honest industry merely jogs along, curiosity flies on Mercury's pinions. Passionate reading not only flies, it skips, but it does so only because it can choose, which is a high intellectual achievement. How do you read the timetable? You skip till you come to your place; then you are indifferent to the whole world and engrossed by your train, its departure, arrival, and connections. The same thing with any formula for the production of the philosopher's stone.

Whatever we read from *intense curiosity* gives us the *model of how we should always read. Plodding along page after page* with an equal attention to each word *results in attention to mere words. Attention* to *words never produces thought*, but very promptly results in distractions, so that an honorable effort is brought to nought by its own ill-advised conscientiousness.[3]

But suppose for a moment the reader reads the question without seeing it, and this is highly probable for the word-reader. If such be the case, the whole paragraph is lost, because there can be no answer unless there is a question.

Note the essentials of the topic sentence in this expository paragraph (again the italics are the author's):

Among the many kinds of material we must find in books, at least *three* are readily distinguished: *happenings, facts* and *principles.* Happenings—the narratives of *what* has *occurred*—concern us in *all forms* of *fiction*, whether as plays, novels, or stories. And *happenings* are a major part of all *history* and *biography.* Throughout such narratives and in almost all *sorts of writing* we encounter *facts* which may lack narrative connection: dates, names, locations, definitions, descriptions of processes. Less concrete than either happenings or facts, and often *harder* to *remember*, are *principles*: the *translation* of *facts into* statements

3. Ernest Dimnet, *The Art of Thinking* (New York: Simon and Schuster, Inc., 1928), 19.

of *law*, the *interpretation* of *happenings* as *cause* and *effect*, or the attempts to explain *human experience* in the *form* of *theories*.[4]

The topic sentence is made to alert the reader; the signal word *three* gives the clue. The body of the paragraph explains what *happenings, facts,* and *principles* are. The reader who knows what to look for will not have to reread this paragraph.

Here is a summary paragraph for this part of the chapter. Will it help you remember what to look for in your reading?

Summary Paragraph

What does the good reader look for as he reads? First, for the only thing that can be gleaned from the printed page, thoughts. Second, the reader looks for action on a wide screen—he moves quickly over the page, getting a bird's-eye-view. Third, he knows the form of discourse, patterns of paragraphs, and structure of sentences so thoroughly that they add to the action of reading by almost literally jumping from the page to meet the reader. Finally, the reader looks with an eye to selection and classification of the kinds of material found in books—happenings, facts, and principles. What the good reader looks for in his reading causes him to think, and indeed, all effective reading is thinking.

Understanding More

The second major area that concerns the reader who wishes to improve (and doubtless few of us are ever far from this problem) is how to comprehend more of what we read and remember it longer.

The first step toward greater comprehension and longer retention is *purpose*—a clear realization of the objectives to be

4. E. Wayne Marjarum, *How to Use a Book* (New Brunswick: Rutgers Univ. Press, 1947), 4.

attained by manner and subject. The skillful reader aims to co-ordinate his purpose with the purpose of the writer, thinking with, and pursuing the same goals that the author had in writing. In an essay entitled, *A Teacher Looks at Reading*, A. B. Herr classifies the purposes of writers under three major divisions:

> (1) to give information—an intellectual operation; (2) to share experiences, sentiments, and convictions—an operation which includes intellectual comprehension but is not complete without emotion, the feeling of having participated; and (3) to persuade, to change options, responses, or habits—an operation whose success depends on emotional acceptance, no matter how intellectual the approach may appear.[5]

The nature of the assignment for work-type material will generally dictate the purpose. Once the purpose has been established the reader will then decide which of the three types of reading he will use: (1) skimming, (2) careful, or (3) intensive, or a combination. If the purpose is to locate information, skimming will suffice; but mastery that demands gathering facts and understanding their interrelationship, forming opinions backed by substantial evidence, might well dictate skimming first—followed by careful or intensive reading.

A second practice for better comprehension and easier retention is to condition the mind for positive rather than negative results. Many readers, faced with a difficult passage or assignment, start by expecting *not* to be able to understand and remember. This prepares the mind psychologically for defeat. Expect to understand and remember, and for a while it is excellent training to speak aloud to one's self: "I am going to remember this after one reading." Would the runner win the race if at the starting gun he said to himself, "I know I can't win"? Would the hurdler clear the hurdle if he said just before he left the ground, "I know I won't clear it"? Purpose plus confidence will, with the reader's help, interact to insure comprehension and retention.

5.   A. B. Herr, "A Teacher Looks at Reading," Alfred Steppernd, *The Wonderful World of Books: Collection of Essays* (Boston: Houghton Mifflin Co., 1953), 83.

A third aid to comprehension and retention is to read with questions in mind. The right questions can result in helping the reader enclose what he is reading with experience or association, thus making information so personal as to make forgetting impossible. What would you have done at the Battle of Thermopylae? Would you have enjoyed walking and talking with Milton as he felt his way along his garden path with his cane? Could the author have stated this rule more clearly? The example seems rather vague, what could I use as a better one? "There is no such thing as an interesting book or assignment"; to paraphrase Emerson, "there are only interested readers." And it might be added that only interesting questions make interested readers. How is this assignment related to the preceding one? Will what I already know about the topic make it easier for me to remember the facts I am now adding? And when a section or chapter is finished, self-recitation questions about main topics and how successfully, or unsuccessfully, the author has presented them will increase your ability to remember more of what you have read.

Retaining what is read is aided by finding some unifying association or significance. Facts and ideas can be very dull, but if some relationship can be established, whether logically or arbitrarily, it can serve as a packaging device and function as a convenient package.

Remembering Longer

Into much of the reading done in school must be introduced the learning skill that always causes students to shudder—memorization. It need not be an awesome word, and you need not fear it. Perhaps you would have a clearer understanding of much that you have to read if your teacher did not try to avoid using it by substituting phrases such as "learn all" or "learn the whole ten rules."

The first step in improving your powers of memory and putting them to work in your reading is to find out the kinds of ideas you remember with less difficulty than others—whether happenings, facts, or principles, and the element in each that helps you remember. Some people remember color, others motion, still others cannot remember numbers when they are spelled out. General U. S. Grant could not remember the names of three consecutive towns he passed while marching, but on a topographical map he could memorize dozens of towns and their location in a matter of seconds. Alexander the Great could not remember the names of some of his close acquaintances, but he could memorize poetry with almost no effort.

Psychologists are generally agreed that each of us has not one memory power but many. By testing whether it is *faces, places, dates, designs, pictures from reality, pictures from imagination, association with the physical or mental world* that we remember more easily, we can find our memory strengths and use them as the association frames upon which to hang what is to be remembered.

One very simple but effective test is to think quickly of some one you met recently. How do you remember him? By what he was doing? By the place where you saw him first? By who was with him? By the color of his shirt or jacket? By some number—books he was carrying, steps forward to shake hands, words spoken? By what he really looked like?—(reality). By what you thought he might have looked like?—(imagination). Which do you remember more distinctly—his handshake? (physical)—or what he said? (mental). Apply the same test to a character you meet in your reading.

When association and memory are not sufficient because the facts to be remembered are so numerous, the reader's last recourse is to take notes. If you own the book you are reading, marginal notes and the designation of important points by some system of marking suited to your purpose and kept consistent can be invaluable.

One of the simplest methods of designating degrees of importance is to use one, two, or three vertical lines: | for important, ‖ for very important, and ⦀ for "must remember." Some students use a (?) question mark to indicate "further study needed"; some use *T* or *Ex.* to signal likely test or examination material. One splendid practice for marginal notes is to write the main thought of a paragraph in a brief question beside the paragraph. Some students try to summarize with such brevity as to include the summary at the end of each paragraph. These marginal exercises are only recommended for a book that is your property; never mark a book that is not your own.

Note-taking on what you read forces you to think and to be constantly alert for the essentials. Such notes can be kept in better order and made available for quick use if taken on 3 × 5 index cards. These can be filed by subject or book for any desired reference or project, and are far more easily arranged than looseleaf notebook material.

A review of summary writing and outlining will afford you two methods of taking notes on what you read. There are, however, two additional types of reading notes sometimes used: (1) question and answer, and (2) word and phrase list. The question and answer method states the question in full and then gives key words or phrases to indicate the answer. For example:

I.   What does a good summary contain?
   A.   Principal ideas
   B.   Author's point of view
   C.   Student's vocabulary

II.   What are the steps in making a summary?
   A.
   B.
   C.

The question and answer method sharpens your attentiveness and enforces the questioning attitude. Once practiced it leads to clear-cut distinctions between major and minor topics.

The word-and-phrase-list form of notes on reading is little more than an unorganized outline. It is used most often for immediate use, such as reviewing quickly for tests. It offers a series of warning signals, reminding the reader what to remember. For example, this chapter:

READING: FASTER WITH MORE UNDERSTANDING

LOOK FOR	*RETENTION*
Bird's-eye-view	Memory powers
Thoughts	Application and
Main topics	association
	Marginal notes
COMPREHENSION	Written notes
Writer's aim	
Questions on material	*INCREASING SPEED*
Happenings	Self-tests
Facts	Conscious purpose
Principles	Hollow triangle
	Mechanics
	Cautions

Note that words indicating principal parts are in italics. The student would probably act wisely to use *Summary, Outline,* or *Question and Answer,* except for more informal and less demanding subject matter.

Reading Faster

The third principal area for improvement in reading has to do with the speed at which you read. It is an established fact that fast readers are more accurate and remember more than slow readers. And, of course, they have the great advantage of saving much time. The slow reader loses his train of thought, and often his place on the page, among words; whereas the fast reader reads several words at a glance and is consequently dealing only in thoughts. There are available many self-tests for measuring your reading speed and comprehension. Your English teacher may be able to provide you one, or perhaps even administer such a test. This should be your first operation. Find out how fast you read at present, and how much you comprehend of what you read. If you have reading difficulties, the test will probably pinpoint areas where specific practices can help.

How do we read? First of all, every reader faces the problem of coordinating the mind and the eye. The mind is capable of receiving ideas much more rapidly than the eye is able to receive and relay them. Thus, the problem of mind-wandering arises. If we do not discipline the mind to remain ready, it escapes to thoughts of ourselves, friends, what we are going to do later— and suddenly we have lost our place on the page. The slower one reads the more difficult it is to control the mind; therefore, rapid reading is training the eye to speed up and the mind to accept the eye's pace.

Our eyes move across the page by a series of quick stops, not in a flowing, even movement. These stops are called fixations, and whether we see one word or several at a fixation determines our speed of reading. The fast reader, who will always remember more of what he reads than the slow reader, makes two or three fixations as he reads the line of print, and he sees groups of words, ideas, and thoughts. The slow reader is usually addicted to interrupting the forward movement across the page to glance backward. This is called "regression" and is a bad and confusing habit resulting from reading without sufficient purpose and speed. The good reader sweeps from the end of the finished line downward and to the beginning of the next with no difficulty; the slow reader will often make two or three false starts on beginning a line, and frequently reread the line just read or skip the one he should read. This, of course, is not completely the fault of the eye. Until the eye and the brain are working together, all these sloppy and fatal habits of reading prevail. Mechanical practices will help, but the determined effort to concentrate on increasing speed and comprehension, and a willingness to make each assignment a practice in better reading habits, will prove your greatest aid.

One mechanical aid to measure your "recognition span," the number of words you see at a fixation, may, however, be recommended. From cardboard or some other semi-stiff material cut out a hollow triangle. Make the base wide enough to take in six or eight words. Place it on the line and move from top to bottom to determine how many words you see at a fixation. It may be used for a few minutes practice each day, or as a test from time to time to measure improvement. Progress may also be noted on a chart on which you can enter the number of pages (of similar type material) that you can read in a 15-minute period. If you are putting serious effort into reading improvement this test should be done weekly.

Careful self-analysis of your own capacities will dictate your methods. Be cautious about developing speed with comprehension. Nervous haste without understanding will produce no beneficial results. Let the purpose determine the speed. Concentrate on correcting the obvious faults of the slow reader, and the increase in speed will usually take care of itself.

Above all else, keep three things in mind. One, that all study problems have as their basis a reading problem. Two, improvement in reading is a lifetime process. Three, if we read, we can become better readers; if we do not read, we become increasingly poorer readers.

Practices for Better Reading

1. Prepare the mind psychologically for positive results.

2. Know the three aims of a good reader:
    a. to concentrate on what is being read,
    b. to remember as much as possible, and
    c. to apply or associate what is read to one's own experience.

3. Know the three general types of reading and the type of material to which each may be profitably applied:
    a. skimming,
    b. careful reading, and
    c. intensive reading.

4. Know that the good reader looks for:
    a. thoughts,
    b. bird's-eye-view,
    c. main topics, and
    d. pattern and structure in picturing ideas.

5. Understand the approaches to better comprehension and retention:
   a. Reading is a conversation with the author.
   b. Remember the purpose for which the reader is reading.
   c. Always read with questions in mind.
   d. Use memory powers to improve retention by association and application.
   e. Make use of written notes.

6. Make a determined effort to increase speed of reading:
   a. Use self-tests for speed and rate of improvement.
   b. Know the mechanical functions of the eye in reading.
   c. Keep in mind the faults of the slow reader.
   d. Know that fast readers remember more of what they read than slow readers.
   e. Discipline the eye to take in more at a fixation.
   f. Remember that speed without understanding is useless.

Looking Back

1. Why is so much emphasis being placed on speed in reading? If a student can absorb the material only by reading at a snail's pace, should he be concerned about reading faster? Why?

2. The acronym to help you remember the four basic types of paragraphs is EDNA: identify the four types and describe them briefly.

3. An important aid to increasing your reading comprehension is to read with specific questions in mind. Tell about three other useful suggestions that were offered in this chapter.

WORDS: HOW TO IMPROVE YOUR KNOWLEDGE OF THEM

True Confessions

1. There is an old joke about a student who looked up the meaning of "to be frugal" and found out that one of the dictionary definitions was "to save." He then used the word in a homework sentence: "When the man fell overboard, he shouted, 'Frugal me!'"

    Have you ever misused a word that way? Tell about it. How could such errors be avoided?

2. What word did you look up in a dictionary lately? Why did you want to know its meaning? How have you used it since you discovered its meaning?

3. A high school senior asked: "Why are teachers always pushing us to use big words? Can't I say the simple word 'cut' or must I use a four-syllable word such as 'laceration'? After all, Ernest Hemingway specialized in words of one syllable, and he was one of America's greatest writers."

    How might a teacher answer that question?

Why Study Words?

The purpose of this word study is to help you increase your vocabulary, adapt it to more meaningful use, and through that improved use, raise your marks. If there seems to be delay in offering suggestions for dictionary use, keeping lists of new words, and putting new words to work, do not be impatient. These are back-door methods necessary for those who somehow miss the excitement of entering word study by the front door, and the front door of word study is interest. W. H. Auden, the poet, recommended that anyone who wants to be a poet should be able to defend his aspiration by saying: "'Because I like to hang around words and overhear them whisper to one another.'"[1]

The Many Qualities of Words

Words are the tools of thinking. Beginning with the grunts and exclamations of our remote ancestors, words, these symbols of thought, have flowered into their many uses to provide man with a history totally different from the lower primates. Writes J. Donald Adams:

> In words are reflected all the delights and miseries of human existence. Words are one of the most living things of man's creation; indeed, one might argue that they have more vitality than anything else we have fashioned. What else is there that seems to lead an independent life? Words do; they acquire strength and lose it; they may, like people, become transformed in character; like certain persons, they may gather evil about them, or like others, prod our wits and lift our hearts.[2]

1. As quoted by John Ciardi, "Manner of Speaking," *Saturday Review* 55 (March 11, 1972): 14.
2. J. Donald Adams, *The Magic and Mystery of Words* (New York: Holt, Rinehart, and Winston, 1963), 36.

How particular sounds came to represent particular things is also part of the fascinating story of words. In Plato's shortest dialogue, *Cratylus*, covering only four pages, Socrates speculates on the origin of words. He suggests that many names indicate the nature of the thing named—some names express rest while others show an affinity for motion. The sound of *l* seems to suggest the *lull* that *lures* toward the *lunar* world of rest. How many words with *l* can you list?—leisure, lullaby, lassitude, lazy—the lengthening *list* makes one *listless*. Over against the rest-inducing *l* stands *r*, suggesting motion—run, race, rowdy, rodeo, rattle, ruin, ripple. Ripple, the last mentioned, suggests that some words echo the sound of the thing for which they stand. (The ripples crept quietly under the over-hanging bank. The brook babbled its protest to the rocks as it raced along).

The Origin of Words

Etymology is the study of the origin and development of a word, says your dictionary, tracing a word as far back as possible. The word etymology comes from two Greek words—*etymon*, meaning "true sense," and *logy*, meaning "the study of." Etymology usually proceeds by the method of linguistic comparisons, indeed, an exciting means of discovering the romance behind our everyday language. Add to this the origin of names, and word study takes on an absorbing and fascinating quality found in few subjects.

Think briefly of several names around you. Perhaps, there is a mountain named Hawk's Peak, another named Candlewood. Long ago the Indians watched the hawks soar above the peak, brushing the sky with their wings, and named the mountain. And having gone to gather pitch pine to light his frontier cabin, substituting the pine torch for candles, the frontiersman named the mountain where he found the candle wood—Candlewood Mountain.

Etymology, begun with the familiar that lies before your very eyes, and extended to your dictionary, will not only enrich your vocabulary, but will make you word conscious and indirectly improve your ability to read with more comprehension and spell more correctly.

To create a picture of the origin of a single word is to journey into a remote past. The evolution of words reaches far back in time, perhaps eighty thousand years. For many thousands of years signs and grunts named things men saw—slowly language evolved from these mere names of concrete things to expressions of abstract ideas.

About four thousand years ago man advanced his evolution of speech and words into a new epoch; he began to write. First he scratched strangely and crudely on stone, perhaps also with a pointed stick in the sand; afterwards on bits of hardened clay, and finally his materials included papyrus, parchment, and paper. How did he begin? Doubtless with a picture. Slowly the picture came to represent an idea. The idea came to be represented by a symbol—a symbol that could be read and uttered. This was a written word.

Ever since the time of Socrates there have been many theories about the origins of words and names. Was the Indian who looked out from his campsite high on the Blue Ridge Mountains naming the beautiful valley below? Was he echoing the sound of earth and sky caressing at the edge of the vast panorama? Or was he raising his arms in awesome devotion to the daughter-of-the-skies? Anyway, the word he made was—Shen-an-doah, Shenandoah. Is there a single valley on the earth more beautifully named? And what of Je-ru-sa-lem—that beautiful, musical word? How came the word—the name—from David's harp or the wind whispering among the promontory rocks?

The Excitement of Words

The excitement of words! A thousand word games, histories, and stories are all about you daily. Do not let the fascination of words be clouded or lost. Every word was in its beginning a stroke of genius. And according to Emerson, "Every word was once a poem." "Uttering a word," said the philosopher Ludwig Wittgenstein, "is like striking a note on the keyboard of the imagination." Words convey most of our ideas and thoughts. Without them we can think only in concrete terms—we can picture an object, a rock, for instance; but we cannot picture an abstraction, such as love. To express the idea of "love" we need words.

The putting together of words to produce distinctive and understandable prose demands sentences that deal quietly and justly with the common feelings of men, and give beauty and loftiness to things of the everyday world—things which, if not lifted up, are sometimes lost in the drab words of grocery lists, small complaints in little language, and repetitions stamped with dullness.

Some of the earth's benefactors came to greatness through their ability to give color, simplicity, enduring strength, and nobility to words. In analyzing the qualities that made Abraham Lincoln great, Benjamin P. Thomas wrote:

Mastery of language may have been that ultimate factor without which he would have failed. For the self-taught man who once would have given all he owned and gone into debt for the gift of lyric utterance had touched the summits of eloquence. Yet this, like his other achievements, had not come by mere chance. Patient self-training, informed reflection, profound study of a few great works of English literature, esteem for the rhythmic beauty that may be coaxed from language, all these had endowed him with the faculty to write well and to speak well, so that at last, when profound emotions deep within him had felt the impulse of new-born nobility of purpose, they had welled forth—and would well forth once more—in imperishable words.[3]

How then can you put your love of words into action—"to write well and to speak well"? There are four steps: use a dictionary, learn the roots from which many words come, learn prefixes and suffixes, and *use* the words you have learned.

3.   Benjamin P. Thomas, *Abraham Lincoln* (New York: Alfred A. Knopf, Inc., 1950), 500.

1. Use a Dictionary

The first step is to make friends with the dictionary, to make it your lifelong companion. The word "dictionary" is derived from the Latin word *dictio,* meaning *to speak,* or *to point out in words*; the dictionary is a book that speaks to us about words. It tells us: a. what are the origins of words, b. how to pronounce them, c. what parts of speech they are, d. how to spell them, e. what their meanings are, f. similar words (synonyms), g. words that have opposite meanings (antonyms). Practice using your dictionary in as thorough a manner as possible. Do not hurry through the entry for the word. Read all the meanings of the word—not merely the first. Try looking at the word *sound* or *round.* The entry for either of these words is very long. You will be surprised to find how many different uses each of these words has.

2. Learn the Roots of Words

The second part of vocabulary improvement is to learn how to examine the parts of words. Many of the words in the English language have three parts: a prefix, a root, and a suffix. If you learn some prefixes, some roots, and a few suffixes, you can multiply your vocabulary rather than merely add to it word by word.

You would benefit more from memorizing a hundred roots and how to use them than from memorizing five thousand individual words. Of the more than six hundred thousand words in our language, almost half come from about eight hundred roots.

The word *root* is apt, for as the root of a tree supplies the means of growth, so does a knowledge of word roots enable your vocabulary to grow. Not only will you improve your knowledge of meaning but also of spelling. So, take the shortcut to word power—learn roots, and how to use them.

All of the words of English have individual histories, all have origins deep in the past and deep in other languages. The two ancient languages that provide the roots for many of our words are Latin and Greek. Ten Latin verbs provide roots for more than two thousand of our own words.

LATIN VERB	MEANING	ROOTS FOR ENGLISH WORDS
capio	take, seize	cap- (cip-) capt- (cept-)
duco	lead	duct- duc-
facio	do, make	fac- (fic-) fact- (fect-)
fero	carry, bear	fer- lat-
mitto	send	mit- mitt- miss-
plico	fold	-plica- plicat- (plect-) (plex-)
pono	place, put	pon- posit-
tendo	stretch	tend- tent-
teneo	have, hold	tene- tent-
specio	observe, see	spec- (spic-) speci- spect-

Notice that the root *tent-* may come from either of two of the Latin verbs. You will need to remember that as you examine words. For example, from which root does re*tent*ion come, and from which root does con*tent*ion come? The difference in the origin of the roots alters the meaning significantly.

As a beginning to your study of roots, try to find three English words that come from each of the ten Latin verbs.

3.   Learn Prefixes and Suffixes

The third part of vocabulary building is to learn prefixes and suffixes. These are the parts added to the beginning (prefix) or to the end (suffix) of the root. They will alter the meaning of the word and so are very important. For example *pre*tend and *in*tend mean rather different things, even though they come from the same root. The prefix has made all the difference.

The following list is of common prefixes and their meanings. It would be very worth your while to memorize this list.

PREFIX	MEANING	EXAMPLE
a, ab	from, away	avert, abstain
a, an	without, not	atheist, anarchist
ad, af, at, ag	to	adhere, affix, attain, aggressive

PREFIX	MEANING	EXAMPLE
ambi	both	ambidextrous
amphi	around	amphitheater
ant, anti	against	antonym, antipathy
ante	before	antedate
cata	down	cataract, catacomb
con, cor, com	with, together	convene, correlate, compare
contra	against	contradict
de	from, down	descend, debase
di	apart	divert, divorce
dia	through	diameter, diagonal
dis	not	disagree, disappear
e, ex	out of, over	evaluate, exponent
em	out	emanate
em	in	embark
en	in	enclose
hyper	above, over	hypercritical
hypo	under	hypodermic
il	not	illegal, illegible
im	in, not	import, impossible
in	not	inactive
ir	not	irresponsible
per	through	permeate
peri	around	perimeter
post	after	postpone, posterity
pre	before	predict, precede
pro	for, forth	pronoun, procession
re	back, again, down	recall, revive, retreat
sub, sup	under	subordinate, suppose
super	over, above	supervise
trans	across	transport, transmit

Now use the prefixes and the roots to create some words. Check your accuracy with your dictionary. For example, check out: complicate, emit, or reception. How many words can you create?

Suffixes usually tell us how the word is to be used rather than telling us something about its meaning. They tell us whether the word is a noun, an adjective, or a verb, or the comparative degree of an adjective: small*er*, small*est*. Two suffixes may be added to a root to create a word, as in aggress*ively*. You should have a working knowledge of the following suffixes.

SUFFIX	HOW WORD WILL BE USED	MEANING	EXAMPLE
-able, -ible	adjective	capable of	digestible, reliable
-ac, -al, -ial	adjective	pertaining to	cardiac, natural, facial
-acy	noun	pertaining to	legacy
-ance, -ence	noun	state of being	abundance, obedience
-ant, -ent	noun	one who does	servant, student
-er, -or	noun	one who does	actor
-ive	adjective or noun	state of being	aggressive, executive
-ish	adjective	the quality of	mannish
-ity	noun	the quality of	humility
-less	adjective	without	sleepless
-ly	adjective or adverb	like	cheerfully, lovely
-ness	noun	state of	goodness
-ry	noun	state of	rivalry
-ion	noun	act of	tension

This list is, by no means, exhaustive. It, at best, merely suggests what kinds of changes suffixes can make in words.

Now use your knowledge of roots, prefixes, and suffixes to create a few words; for example, missive, permissive, permission, remission, conduct, conductor.

4.   Use New Words

The fourth and final part of vocabulary building is to use the new words you have learned. Incorporate them into your writing for class and into your everyday speech. Without use you will lose the words you have worked to learn.

To make the words familiar friends, strive to memorize them and their meanings. Use new word lists or, far better, new word cards. You may keep a list of new words in your notebook along with their meanings; especially a list of basic vocabulary words that apply to a particular subject, such as biology, chemistry, history, or geometry. The word should be written with the definition that is directed toward the subject. If there are synonyms that help fix the meaning in your mind, they should be written in a column to the right of the definition as here shown:

NEW WORD   DEFINITION   SYNONYM

The card system for new words is, however, greatly recommended. Most students find it more workable and adaptable. Vocabulary builder cards can be bought, and are highly advisable for vocabulary study of a foreign language; but for your English vocabulary, a great deal of enjoyment can come from building your own. Equip yourself with the smallest index cards you can buy—1½ × 3 or 3 × 5. Keep them handy as you read or study. When you come upon a new word, write it on the front of the card. On the back write the definition or definitions, and a synonym or two. Carry half a dozen or more cards with you, or display them on your desk, until you have put them in your working vocabulary; that is, until you are using them in conversation and in your writing. This will seldom take more than three of four days. The cards may then be filed alphabetically or by subject vocabulary. Just a few weeks of practice and the new word cards become second nature. They can be studied while riding or walking to and from classes, waiting for a bus, and at myriad other odd moments, usually lost and lamented. Put the new word card system to work to improve your vocabulary and your marks.

Practices for Vocabulary Improvement

1. Use your dictionary. When you come upon a new word, a new use for an old word, a word that you think you know but are not sure of, reach for your dictionary. Always keep it within easy reach. Some of your more technical textbooks may have a glossary at the front or back. The glossary will provide the meanings of technical words pertaining to the particular subject, and may also supply meanings for new scientific words— so new they are not in your dictionary. Technical words, explanatory concepts, definitions, and rules of special meaning may be conveniently arranged in the front or back of your algebra, biology, chemistry, literature, or history textbook. Your dictionary study may lead you to other helpful books: *A Dictionary of Modern English Usage,* H. W. Fowler; Fernald's *Synonyms and Antonyms*; and Roget's *Thesaurus of English Words and Phrases.* The word *thesaurus* comes from the Greek word meaning treasury. Indeed, all dictionaries are treasuries; storehouses not for money but for information. The thesaurus may be purchased in economically priced paperbacks. Why not add a treasury or two to your study desk?

2. Avoid word blindness. You use some words daily without knowing their full meaning. Some words that you read as part of assignments would add much to your understanding of the subject if you really knew them. Try these practices for teaching yourself the exact meanings of familiar words for which you have only vague definitions. a. Begin seeing the word whenever you come upon it. Study how it is used by others. b. Question your own use in comparison with others. c. Use your dictionary to find out if you are getting the most out of the familiar word. d. Apply a specific mean-

ing that will make your algebra, geometry, social studies, easier for you to understand. Vagueness is the curse attending many of the words we use without really knowing.

3. Become a word surgeon. Learn to dissect words into their parts—prefix, root, and suffix. Study word parts until a glance reveals the pattern of the word—whether it is single root, built upon prefix, root, suffix, two roots, or some other combinations. Divide *autobiography, bibliography, pandemonium,* and *transmutation* into word parts. A working knowledge of a few fundamental parts, keen powers of observation, and conscientious practice, is the fast way to add new words to your vocabulary.

4. Put new words to work. Insure a working knowledge by recording each new word along with definition and synonym. A sentence of your own, using the word, is also helpful. New word lists and new word cards are recommended ways of keeping satisfactory records. A word is part of your working vocabulary when you can pronounce it, spell it, and use it in both conversation and writing. New words will not remain alive unless they are allowed to work.

5. Use the unlimited word-world of fascination that surrounds you on all sides. John Ruskin defined genius as "a superior power of seeing." Why not use this definition to give yourself the quality of genius in word study? Exercise that "superior power of seeing" to enjoy for the first time place names, your own names, words derived from people's names, trade names, words that name our foods, our days, our weeks, our months, our seasons, and how about your own last name? Make a game of improving your vocabulary and the ability to use that vocabulary. "To carry the feelings of childhood into the powers of manhood," said Coleridge, "to combine the child's sense of wonder and novelty with the appearance which every day for years has rendered familiar, that is the character and privilege

of genius. . . ." Keep "the child's sense of wonder and novelty" for your word study.

Looking Back

1. One of the best ways to broaden your vocabulary is to consult a dictionary frequently in order to find the meaning of unfamiliar words. What are the three other suggestions for expanding your word knowledge that were mentioned in this chapter?

2. On Scholastic Aptitude Tests, you are asked to identify the opposite meanings of specific vocabulary words. For example:

   antebellum: a. relative   b. after the war   c. a ringing   sound   d. outrageous   e. absurd

   How would you go about picking the correct answer, assuming you did not know the meaning of antebellum? What answers would you be looking for if the vocabulary test words were *biped, retrogress, matriarchy*?

3. "Some of the earth's benefactors came to greatness through their ability to give color, simplicity, enduring strength, and nobility to words."

   The above quotation comes from Chapter 11 and will, no doubt, remind you of Churchill, Lincoln, and other great wordsmiths who have been mentioned in this book. Can you name three contemporaries who use language skillfully? They may write for newspapers, create lyrics for rock 'n roll groups, or be your pen pals. Bring examples of their work that you can share with the class.

12

WRITTEN WORK: THE PRODUCT AND ITS PACKAGE

True Confessions

1. When your teacher returns a graded composition to you, filled with red-ink corrections and bearing a low mark, do you examine it carefully or quickly conceal it from the gaze of your classmates? How can teachers make sure that students are profiting from their comments and corrections?

2. When the English class started, Mr. Snyder began to distribute sheets for a brief writing assignment on Poe's "The Cask of Amontillado." "Will this count?" several students asked.

   Is it likely that you would have asked the question? What answer does an experienced teacher usually make to that question?

3. "I know that the composition I submitted was sloppy in its appearance, but I think that teachers should be more concerned with content than with erasures, penmanship, and similar nonsense. I'm going to complain about my failing mark."

   Tell why you do or do not support such a protest.

The Nature of the Product

Of the several skills you will develop in educating yourself—listening, reading, speaking, thinking, and writing—the one that will give your teachers the widest range for measuring your ability and achievements will be your writing. It is also the skill that you will use without much help from the teacher, for most of your written work will be done in class to answer questions (and the teacher cannot help) or out of class when you are on your own.

Certain classroom activities tend to make the other skills cooperative practices between teacher and student. The teacher can design lectures and tests to help you improve your span and depth of listening. Emphasis on the nature of various reading assignments and help in underlining and finding the important facts are usually a part of classroom activity. The teacher will frame class questions and discussions to aid you in developing your capacity to think. And in speaking, if you are inarticulate and have difficulty in putting your recitation in order, the teacher can fill in a word and direct your statements into positive channels.

Beyond the drills provided in the fundamentals—spelling, handwriting, punctuation and capitalization, structure and pattern—in your English classes your ability and skill in writing will almost always be judged as a finished product. This judgment will, fortunately, or unfortunately, affect what your teachers in every school subject think of your work; because it is in writing that you offer them what you have learned. Not only is your written work the measure of what you have learned, but it reveals more of your character, your willingness to pursue excellence or accept mediocrity, than perhaps any other of your school work. It is, in fact, the most important product that you have to sell. You sell it, not for dollars and cents, but for a grade. As with any other product, the quality product brings the quality price.

The pricing does not begin with the term paper or the big test or theme. Your saleable written product begins with the daily paper, be it two sentences, a list of ten words, or five problems in mathematics. It includes not only English papers, as many students mistakenly think, but laboratory reports, all test papers, daily papers, weekly themes, book reviews, term papers, and in college a thesis of perhaps from ten to twenty thousand words.

The *primary purpose* of all written work is to impart information or develop thought. The *primary requirement* of all written work is that it be: (1) interesting, (2) mechanically correct, and (3) attractive. Of course, the quality of a group of problems or word list is measured only by the degree of correctness and attractiveness; attractiveness being accomplished by neatness and arrangement. A list of ten words strung across the page, unnumbered, illegibly written, means something quite different to the teacher than does a list numbered down the page in a straight column, neat and legible—reflecting care. Five problems arranged on a paper for symmetry and neatness, each problem distinctly numbered, each answer marked for easy identification, bring a better price than the indifferent, sloppy paper, even though both papers might have the correct answers.

Certain obligations are basic to the gifted and the ungifted writer alike: (1) For each written assignment the writer is obligated to make the necessary study and inquiry to have a working knowledge of the subject about which he is writing. (2) All students are obligated to present information in a fluent and effective vocabulary, coherent and unified sentence and paragraph structure, and the greatest degree of mechanical perfection possible. (3) And most important of all is the moral obligation never to try to pass off thoughtless, trite, boring, and sloppy written work with no aim beyond that of getting by. Print these three basic obligations on cards, and post them at the front of your desk. Read them before you start your written assignments.

All effective written composition presupposes having something to say. There is among students the feeling that to be seen on record is sufficient. Being seen on record merely means filling up space with writing. The space-filler is not infrequently the same person who has developed a very affected, decorative handwriting that looks attractive at a distance but that is almost impossible to read. The space-filler is also easily identified by a crude way of repeating generalities, adding to the teacher's eternal burden of having to read worthless, cut-rate, and meaningless rubbish. Not so the students who accept the basic obligations as the moral law of written work. They have thought clearly before they begin to write. They have written clearly and meaningfully. They have written with such interest that it cannot be hidden from the teachers who read their papers.

If your written work is not clearly understandable, and in the form of which you are capable, you are either lazy or affected; and your teacher will detect it in the first paper you write. If you write on a subject about which you have no sound knowledge, you are a dishonest pretender. If you know your subject but do not bother to express your thoughts in the best possible form, you are indifferent and irresponsible. Thus, the whole character of the writer is revealed. While still in school, the mark you receive on written work is in many ways a grade measurement of you as a person.

Writing Regular Themes

Regular themes are given this designation to distinguish them from what are usually called research or term themes, because a major element in the latter is gathering necessary material. Regular themes, as they concern us here, could be defined as written composition that requires more than a paragraph or two. Indeed, all themes fall generally into two classes, either a composition of ideas or a composition of images.

The composition of ideas deals with relating information and expounding thought. It would include what is usually classified as expository and argumentative writing, such as essays, long examination answers, etc. Themes growing out of history and science assignments would fall in this class.

The theme of images is generally what would be expected as an assignment associated with an English course, although in advanced English courses themes of criticism and explanation would fall in the classification of ideas. The composition of images deals with narrative and descriptive writing, and may take the form of story, description, poetry, or drama.

Four Steps in Theme Writing

This is not to imply that all students are supposed to become instant, talented writers, possessing unusual creative ability. Whatever your talents, you can improve your writing of themes by following four steps: (1) Choosing the subject or, if assigned by the teacher, deciding upon the point of view. (2) Making an outline; studying, and revising the outline. (3) Writing the first copy, making outline revisions if necessary. (4) Writing the final copy.

The subject you choose to write on can influence in many ways the mark you get. Students often make the mistake of choosing one of these four dangerous types of topics: (1) One that is too big—*Living in the Country* rather than *Old Fence Posts*. (2) A topic outgrown after third grade—*What I Did Last Summer* rather than *City Noises*. (3) A topic that is too personal and in poor taste—*My New Car* rather than *A Maine Countryman's Model T*. (4) A topic too controversial about which you have a hearsay opinion rather than information—*Why We Should Not Salute the Flag in School* rather than *The Meaning of Patriotism*.

The troubles arising from choosing a topic that is too big are immediately evident. Nothing worthwhile can be said in six hundred or a thousand words on a topic that would require a volume for intelligent coverage. The big topic for a short theme usually ends in generalizations reflecting the writer's lack of information and forcing the teacher to reread stale and tired facts known by everyone.

Childish and personal topics are generally chosen to avoid any real thinking. Many students have the mistaken idea that six hundred words of drivel, which they themselves could scarcely read without embarrassment, on *What I Did* or *What I Think* or *My New Boat*, will satisfy the word requirements and perhaps get them a passing grade. However, a personal experience that can be used for illustration or example is much to be desired—well thought out and simply presented.

Controversial topics quickly lose all objectivity and become subject to personal feelings. Other people do not necessarily share your feelings and prejudices. The teacher grading your paper would not consciously give a lower grade for ideas with which he was not in agreement, but it is wise to remember that human nature is never solely divorced from a judgment.

If the topic is assigned, you have no problems; if not, there are intelligent approaches to selecting a topic. One excellent approach is to use the index of a subject that interests you. Suppose you are fond of Dr. Albert Einstein as a person. By checking the index of a biography of Dr. Einstein, or some of his writings, you might come upon the topics: *personal life, family, ideas on teaching, close friends.* If you choose the topic *Thoughts on Teaching*, further reference to Dr. Einstein's writings would give you the basic information. If it then appeared too broad, you might further narrow it to *Dr. Einstein's Thoughts on Teaching Loyalty*, or some other narrow topic. The index, however, is always a good place to start.

In selecting a topic for image composition, choose from the world immediately before you. You will write a better paper and get a higher grade for a description of a gnarled and ancient sycamore tree outside your window than for a storm at sea that you have not experienced.

The second progression toward a perfect theme is an outline.
Perhaps you have had the experience of writing a paragraph and
then remembering something you wish you had included; not
too important, but significant enough to have added to the unity
and contributed to the completeness of the thought. Questions
before you write can save you much regret and rewriting. Since
the paragraph requires definite pattern and structure, as well as
content, the questions for it become doubly important. Use the
following as beginners, but add your own: (1) Do I have a complete mental blueprint of what this paragraph is to contain? (2)
What topic sentence do I want to convey the topic clearly to my
reader? (3) What paragraph pattern will best develop the topic?
(4) Will my arrangement of ideas lead naturally from main to
supporting ideas? (5) Will my choice of words make my meaning
clear? (6) Will this paragraph contain only the material necessary
to picture the thought or answer completely? (7) Will it be judged
as distinctive quality writing or muddled generalization that is
devoid of value? (8) Will my concluding statement (summary
sentence) convince my reader of my ability to control, condense,
and keep meaningful structure to the end?

It might surprise and even annoy you that a simple paragraph
demands such planning. Perhaps incentive to undertake these
practices may come from the realization that you will probably
be marked on hundreds of single paragraph test answers before
you finish your schooling. It might also be remembered that
whether you write a two or ten thousand-word theme, the total
merit will be measured by the quality of the sentence first, and
the paragraph next.

If it is necessary to outline (blueprint orally) even a paragraph,
good common sense says that a composition of any length will
not fall into order without an outline. The outline should be made
on 3 × 5 index cards, and only main topics should be recorded
first. After the main topics have been shuffled into the order that
will produce the best emphasis, coherence, and unity, the supporting topics may then be outlined. The nature of the theme
will dictate the order of the outline—chronological, numerical,
alphabetical, place, or some other logical order that you have
devised to fit the topic.

Do not be afraid to spend some time on the outline. It will be saved later on the writing, and the product will be more orderly and complete. Many professional writers spend as much time outlining as they spend in actual writing. You can train yourself to outline orally as you go to and from school, or while you are at some physical exercise. This will save you much time. One writer of academic books outlines each chapter while chopping wood.

Even though you might change the outline somewhat after you start to write, outlining one or two themes will convince you of its many advantages. It prevents mistakes in the selection and arrangement of material and insures a sensible proportion of main and contributing ideas. One of the greatest advantages to outlining is that it leads to the discovery of new ideas, new ways to illustrate a point, and a sense of unity totally new to many young writers.

A careful examination of the completed outline is always helpful. Here again, questions are a good method of testing whether or not the outline does what you expect of it: (1) Will the outline move the theme directly forward and hold the interest of the reader? (2) Is the outline sufficiently planned and clear for the reader to see it beneath the content? (3) Is the outline free of contradictions and repetitions? (4) Does the outline unite main topics in such a way as to make the message of the whole theme possible in a sentence or two, and certainly not more than a brief paragraph?

The outline thus examined, you are ready for the third step in theme writing: to write the first draft of the composition. Three practices governing this writing will prove most helpful: (1) Leave every other line for changes and corrections. (2) Do not write carelessly, even though it is a first draft. (3) Write rapidly and without interruption.

Try to make your first draft look as nearly like the final product as possible. The accomplishments of each step add up to make each succeeding one less difficult; and even though the major concern of the first draft is to get the ideas in order, mechanics of writing should not be neglected. Careless mistakes have habit-forming effects and are likely to show up in the final copy. Some students write a first draft so sloppily as to be totally worthless. These are the people who usually write a first, a second, and a third copy. This is a waste of time—actually it is time spent developing bad writing habits.

Many students mistakenly believe that writing slowly results in a more thorough job. This is not true. Rapid writing gives a spontaneity that will add life to your composition. Rapidity will also give your writing a flowing movement forward, whereas slow writing will move only by jerks. Rapid writing may also dictate changes in your outline that will improve your theme. Do not be afraid to make such changes, for blind affection to the outline can cause stiff and lifeless spots in your composition. Rapid writing makes the work of revision for the final draft little more than correcting errors in mechanics. The slow writer who has struggled over words, crossed out words, confused sentence constructions, and fragmentized ideas by changes finds revision a major job, equivalent to rewriting the whole theme.

The fourth and final step in good composition writing is the production of the final copy. If possible, have a time lapse between the working draft and the final copy. This period for generally thinking over and around the topic will usually result in ideas to clear up difficult spots, in decisions over choice of words, and in the detection of mechanical mistakes made in the first draft.

In the final draft be concerned for the format and general appearance of the paper. Question the use of modifiers. Unless they make a positive contribution, remove them. Ask yourself what your reaction would be if you were the teacher reading and grading the paper. If you can answer this question sincerely, your mark will probably reflect your sincerity and your teacher's appreciation for that rare person—the student who has a "sense of pride in his work" and is willing to expend the energy necessary to put it into effect.

The Nature of the Package

Nothing in a teacher's experience is more rewarding than to receive a written paper of such neatness and quality as to wish that it did not end. On the other side of the card, it is equally true that nothing can cause the teacher so much frustration, such feeling of ineffective teaching, and such painful exasperating waste of time as a paper that shows concern for neither form nor content.

The trite and the ordinary, the mediocre and the humdrum, the boring and the unorganized, reveal a total indifference to clarity, form, style, and quality. Neglect of grammar, spelling, punctuation, vocabulary, and legibility stamps the writer as one whose chief aim is to get by and whose highest standard of measurement is accepted incompetence. From this the teacher can easily judge that completely lacking in the writer's character is any element of appreciation for excellence or even an honest desire to be one's better self.

"But," you reply, "I can't write more legibly." There are many students who expect the teacher to accept this as a valid reason for lack of neatness and order. Is the teacher supposed to go on trying to decipher an impossible mess, to give proper consideration to illegible content, and show sympathy and pity? The answer is No! It is the responsibility of the student to write in such a way that his or her work is easily read and understood. Anything less than this should not even be accepted by the teacher.

Excellence, like courtesy, manners, and thoughtfulness, has become somewhat old-fashioned from lack of use. Since you will hear "minimum requirement" and "permissible" so often to describe what is acceptable, we might pause to examine this beautiful word "excellence," lest it miss being a part of your vocabulary; and more important, a part of your philosophy of life.

"What is excellent is permanent," wrote Emerson. "But how does this relate to something as simple as the way I write a daily quiz paper?'' you ask. Each paper you write confronts you with dealing poorly with yourself and producing the "minimum" or "permissible," or dealing wisely with yourself and producing "excellence." Assuming that you have accepted your responsibility for gathering the required information, excellence goes beyond this and is a part of presentation.

Have you ever had a teacher hold up one of your papers to the class and remark on its order, neatness, and the ease with which it can be graded? This makes up what is generally referred to as the format of the paper. Here are some of the little considerations that can give the format of your written work the quality of excellence.

Do you follow regulations? At the beginning of a course, teachers often lay down certain requirements to be followed during the year: name of student in a particular place on the paper, paper folded or not folded, title in the middle of the first line, quiz questions copied on paper, a line skipped between answers, all answers written in complete sentences, all numbers of questions written to the left of the red margin on the paper, a line omitted between French or Latin sentences to allow for corrections, answers to problems in mathematics underlined and designated *Ans.* for easy recognition. These are only a few of the many elements that go into making your product more attractive by approaching excellence.

Does your work reveal a sense of pride in presentation that cannot be hidden, regardless of whether or not all your answers are correct and your thinking clear? If the assignment is a six hundred-word essay, do you crudely jot down the number of words at the end of each page, finally reaching, for you, the great climax of 608, an insult to your reader. Is your paper as neat as you can possibly make it, or is it in pencil when asked for in ink, and in your illegible scribble that you mistakenly believe can be read by others because you can decipher it? What of the student who, writing on the laws of Hammurabi, misspells Hammurabi in the title of his paper and then alternates between correct and incorrect for the remainder of the paper? What of the person who brings his paper a day late or even an hour late? What of the American history student who, assigned a three thousand-word theme, turns in a disorganized fifteen hundred words, and asked "Why?" by his teacher, replies, "I guess I wasn't interested enough." How very sad! What was lacking?— a sense of pride—without which there is no excellence. For excellence is reaching beyond the little self, going beyond the narrow circumference that stifles and retards the lesser and the average.

It is all very simple. If you accept the "minimum" as a standard, you will get a minimum mark. If you require excellence of yourself, you will get an excellent mark. The same reflections will be mirrored in life after you have completed your studies. Unless your sense of pride demands excellence of you, you might be lucky and make an exciting sale or bring in a big account, but the way you write the report will reveal your true character. If you are not promoted, the answer is within you. You need not ask your employer, "Why?"

Improving Your Writing

Many students misunderstand the basic purpose of theme assignments, and as a result miss the most important contribution that such assignments make to their education. The primary purpose is not a grade, although one should always strive to get the best grade possible. The first objective is to help the student gain proficiency in writing; this can only be achieved if the criticisms given by the teacher are carefully noted and if a sincere effort is made not to repeat the same shortcomings again and again.

If you can remember your last theme grade, but do not know the specific weaknesses or strengths that brought about the grade, you are among those who miss the purpose of theme assignments. When a theme is returned to you, keep it in your notebook. When your next theme is assigned, check your weaknesses from the last one before you start to write. A list of types of mistakes and shortcomings and the frequency with which they occurred on successive themes offers graphic incentive for improvement.

By studying the mistakes you make frequently on two or three themes, you can make yourself an improvement chart to fit your needs. It might appear as follows, although its categories would be tailored to your needs:

IMPROVEMENT CHART FOR WRITTEN WORK

TYPE OF MISTAKES	NUMBER OF TIMES OCCURRING					
	1st Wk.	2nd Wk.	3rd Wk.	4th Wk.	5th Wk.	6th Wk.
Spelling	13	10	9	7	4	0
Punctuation						
Points Off for Lack of Neatness	10	5	0	0	0	0
Sentence Faults						
Poor Paragraph Construction Topic Sentence						
Development						
Arrangement						
Summary Sentence						
Vocabulary Word Choice						
Lack of Clarity						
Affectation						
Mark Received						

(continued)

Overall Criticism Teacher's Comments	First Week
	Second Week
	Third Week
	Fourth Week
	Fifth Week
	Sixth Week

Certainly, there are few among us who do not enjoy evidence of self-improvement. The improvement chart, listing your particular shortcomings, can be used to encourage and record your improvement. If your particular faults can be pinpointed, it will be wise to include them specifically rather than under a general entry. For example, if you make apostrophe and semicolon mistakes more often than others, make individual entries for these under punctuation. Your teachers could probably give valuable help in preparing your chart.

Teachers also can give valuable help if you go to your teacher after class with a paper in hand and ask for extra help. Ask the teacher to show you how to express more clearly what you have tried to say in your paper. In this way you will see how better to arrange your topic or better to express yourself about your topic. If you do not go with paper in hand, your teacher will be glad to help you, but may supply personal examples. It is more helpful to have the examples come from your own paper; you will understand them better and be better able to apply the lessons you learn to your other writing. Going to ask help from your teacher with your work in hand also will show him that you honestly wish to improve and are not there merely in an effort to "butter him up" and make him like you better.

How to Judge Quality

Whether written work takes the form of a single sentence to answer a question, a simple paragraph, or a long theme, the primary requirements are demanded of the writer. Perhaps one of the best methods of producing quality writing is to always approach it with questions, and judge it by questions when it is written.

Ask yourself the following questions about the next one- or two-sentence answers you write. Use these only as beginners, and add questions of your own. Make them progressively demanding until you feel that you have acquired the ability to sense and produce quality answers, and to detect and avoid worthless quantity. Can I start my answer by restating the idea of the question, and thereby make it easy for the reader to mark my paper? Will I carefully avoid using a pronoun to replace the subject of the question? Does this answer contain the fewest number of words possible to make a quality answer? Is this a generalization that does not answer the question, but is a dishonest attempt to get by, and which the teacher will detect immediately? These four questions can change the nature both of the answers you write for tests, and of the themes you write. Copy each on a 3 × 5 index card, and keep them on your desk until you have memorized them. Ask your teacher if you can keep them before you as you take quizzes and tests.

Suggestions for Improving Written Work

1. Written work reveals ability, desire, and character. It is the most important product you have to offer in exchange for a grade.

2. The primary requirement of all written work is that it be presented in: a. an interesting, b. a mechanically correct, and c. attractive manner.

3. Judge the quality of written composition by questioning its parts, content, and presentation.

4. Observe closely the three basic obligations of all students toward written work:
   a. Must have a working knowledge of the subject.
   b. Must present the material in the best possible form and structure.
   c. Must avoid the habit of passing off inferior work in the hopes of getting by.

5. Excellence is the only real quality of written work that is permanent. Excellence in packaging the product (putting written work in an attractive, correct, and neat form) comes from a sense of pride in one's work.

6. Adopt practices that will reveal weaknesses and inspire improvement. Beginning with the four steps in good composition writing, plot your own methods for adding quality and completeness.

Looking Back

1. In deciding on a theme for your Hygiene class, four titles come to mind:
   a. "Maintaining Good Health"
   b. "Acne: Avoiding It and Treating It"
   c. "A Diet That Worked for Me"
   d. "My Uncle's Heart By-Pass Operation"
   Which one would you select? Why? Which is the poorest choice you could have made? Why?

2. In this chapter, four steps in theme writing are discussed:
   a. Pick the best topic
   b. Prepare an outline
   c. Write a first draft
   d. Write a final copy
   Which is the most important step?

3. The opening sentence of this chapter is: "Of the several skills you will develop in educating yourself—listening, reading, speaking, thinking, and writing—the one that will give your teachers the widest range for measuring your ability and achievements will be your writing."

   Tell whether you agree with the statement. Why?

   Select one of the other skills and explain why that one is the most significant for the career you are planning.

13

WRITTEN WORK: STYLE AND USAGE

True Confessions

1. Do you remember Winston Churchill's famous reference to "wounds, unrelenting labor, perspiration, and weeping"? Of course you don't, because Churchill used "blood, toil, sweat, and tears" in his stirring speech to his countrymen.

   Why all the fuss over Churchill's choice of words? Did they really matter? Why? What makes one slogan more memorable than another?

2. Some years ago a gifted copywriter at an advertising agency prepared a sample ad for Ivory soap. In two hundred words he told about the "unique saponification" of Ivory, and how it was engineered to stay atop the water "during one's ablutions." His boss studied the results, then drew a red line through the whole article and replaced it with two words: "It floats!"

   Was the boss' revision an improvement? Tell why?

3. Have you ever uttered sentences similar to those below?
   a. "They say it will rain today."
   b. "He's a Communist, they say, who always favors the Russians over our own country."
   c. "They say she's a terrible mother who actually neglects her children."

What's wrong with such statements? Why do people use them, nevertheless?

Models of Good Style

Written work is critical to your success in school. You cannot escape it—you must write not only in English class, but also in history, science, math, and foreign language classes. Now that we have examined theme writing in some detail, let us turn to the examination of style and usage.

Do pomposity, ostentation, pretentiousness, and ornamentation—fringed with the gingerbread of garbled and garish vocabulary—produce the word pictures that give meaning and understanding to our thoughts? Are not, rather, clarity, simplicity, sincerity, and order—whose by-product is beauty—the things for which we aim? Is this not the pattern of all deathless utterances that are our heritage and our models?

Let's examine what some of the world's great thinkers have written to see how their prose works. Thucydides, the Greek historian, writing a history of the Peloponnesian War, wrote in "such a way," said Plutarch, "as to make his hearer a spectator." Here is the beginning paragraph of Thucydides' description of the deadly plague that ravaged Athens in 429 B.C., carrying away half the population of the city, among whom was the city's foremost leader—Pericles. Note the simplicity of the words used. Not a single technical or medical term appears in the whole three-page description of the disease, yet doctors are able to diagnose the epidemic from symptoms so clearly described. Here follows a single paragraph:

Words indeed fail one when one tries to give a general picture of this disease; and as for the sufferings of individuals, they seemed almost beyond the capacity of human nature to endure. Here in particular is a point where this plague showed itself to be something quite different from ordinary diseases: though there were many dead bodies lying about unburied, the birds and animals that eat human flesh either did not come near them or, if they did taste the flesh, died of it afterwards. Evidence for this may be found in the fact that there was a complete disappearance of all birds of prey: they were not to be seen either round the bodies or anywhere else. But dogs, being domestic animals, provided the best opportunity of observing this effect of the plague.[1]

Sophocles, listed always among the world's greatest dramatists, has the following description of man at the end of the first scene in his play, *Antigone*:

> There are many wonderful things, but none more wonderful than man. Over the whitecaps of the sea he goes, driven by the stormy winds, topped by the towering waves; and the Earth, oldest of the gods, eternal and tireless, he wears away, turning furrows with his plow year after year. He snares the lighthearted birds and the wild beasts of the fields, and he catches in his nets the fish of the sea, man forever resourceful. He tames the animals that roam the meadows and mountains, yoking the shaggy horses and the powerful bulls. And he has learned the use of language to express wind-swift thought, and he has mastered the art of living with other men in addition to the conquest of nature. Skillfully he meets the future; although he has found no escape from death, he has discovered release from painful diseases. His ingenuity results in evil as well as good; when he respects his country's laws and justice he deserves honor; but may the arrogant man, untrue to his city, never come to my hearth or share my thoughts.[2]

In the corridor of the library of Cambridge University hangs a small frame, enclosing a short speech of two hundred eighty-seven words. Under the frame is a placard with the inscription: THE NOBLEST PROSE EVER WRITTEN. The speech is:

> Fourscore and seven years ago our fathers brought forth on this continent a new nation, conceived in liberty, and dedicated to the proposition that all men are created equal.
>
> Now we are engaged in a great civil war, testing whether that

1.   Thucydides, Book 2, 50. As translated by Rex Warner, *Thucydides, The Peloponnesian War* (Baltimore: Penguin, 1954), 125.
2.   Sophocles, *Antigone*, ll. 333–373. As translated by Walter R. Agard, *The Greek Mind* (Princeton: D. Van Nostrand Co. Inc., 1957), 143.

nation, or any nation so conceived and so dedicated, can long endure. We are met on a great battle-field of that war. We have come to dedicate a portion of that field as a final resting-place for those who here gave their lives that that nation might live. It is altogether fitting and proper that we should do this.

But, in a larger sense, we cannot dedicate—we cannot consecrate—we cannot hallow—this ground. The brave men, living and dead, who struggled here, have consecrated it far above our poor power to add or detract. The world will little note nor long remember what we say here, but it can never forget what they did here. It is for us, the living, rather, to be dedicated here to the unfinished work which they who fought here have thus far so nobly advanced. It is rather for us to be here dedicated to the great task remaining before us—that from these honored dead we take increased devotion to that cause for which they gave the last full measure of devotion; that we here highly resolve that these dead shall not have died in vain; that this nation, under God, shall have new birth of freedom; and that government of the people, by the people, for the people, shall not perish from the earth.[3]

On November 19, 1863, a national cemetery was being dedicated at Gettysburg, Pennsylvania, where during the first three days of the previous July, thousands of soldiers had died. Senator Edward Everett was the principal speaker at the dedication. He dealt with concepts of government, the evolution of democracy, and many other profound abstractions for an hour and fifty-five minutes. The world has forgotten what he said, but it remembers Lincoln's Gettysburg Address. Why? Because seldom in history have words been guided by the mind to produce such clarity, simplicity, sincerity, and ordered beauty.

As we turn to look at the uses to which words can be put, the attributes they take on, and how you can make them work best for you, keep constantly in mind the four qualities found in the models just observed: (1) clarity, (2) simplicity, (3) sincerity, and (4) order—which by arrangement produce beauty. These must stand guard over whatever you speak or write; these must be

---

3.   Abraham Lincoln, *The Collected Writings of Abraham Lincoln,* ed. Ray P. Baslen, 9 vols. (New Brunswick: Rutgers Univ. Press, 1953), 7:23.

the primary elements of your style; these must be the qualities that your teachers, your readers, and your listeners find as you express your thoughts.

Clarity

To put it simply, clarity is saying exactly what you mean to say. Be aware of the denoted and the connoted meanings of words. Denoted meanings are the primary, explicit definitions that a dictionary gives. Connoted meanings are the ones that have, through custom and use, come to be associated to a word. When you use a word, all the denotations and connotations will cluster around it, ready to confuse an unwary reader.

In a recent English class a teacher asked his students to write and punctuate the sentence, "When the car went out of control, it struck the pole." A foreign student who was aware of the meaning of pole as in North Pole, but did not know the connoted meaning of pole as in telephone pole, was hopelessly confused. His confusion is humorous, the next example was costly.

Once, a jury, although convinced of a doctor's negligence, failed to award damages to the plaintiff in a civil suit, because they had misunderstood when the lawyer had claimed that the doctor's negligence was so bad as to be criminal. The jury thought, because they had heard the lawyer give utterance to the word criminal, that even though they were deciding a civil suit, if they returned a verdict in favor of the plaintiff, the defendant would be labeled a criminal and be required to go to jail. The jury did not want the doctor to suffer a jail sentence since, although they thought he had been negligent, they felt that the trial and civil suit were suffering enough, and so they returned a verdict in favor of the doctor. They misunderstood, because of the connotations of that one word, criminal, one of the thousands of words that were spoken at the trial.[4]

4. Louis Nizer, *My Life in Court* (Garden City, N.Y.: Doubleday and Co., Inc., 1961), 379.

Do choose your words carefully—you may not lose a court case, but you may lose points on an essay because of poor word choice.

Try a little practice at examining connotations. Examine the word *mark*.

MEANING	USE
Denoted:	
to make a mark (verb)	Mark your notebook for easy identification.
a line, dot, etc. (noun)	Who put the mark on the desk?
Connoted:	
to wait	He will mark time until summer.
a sign or indication	The ability to listen is the mark of a civilized man.
to listen, heed	Mark my words, he will not return.
a sign of evil	He is cursed with the mark of Cain.
a standard of quality	This paper is not up to the mark.
importance, distinction	The chairman is a man of mark.
impression	He left his mark on his students.
a guide or point of reference	The harbor lights were a mark for fliers.
a target	He did not hit the mark.
an aim, goal	The mark of the campaign was to raise six thousand dollars.
a nautical term	Bits of leather indicated the marks on the sounding line. Samuel Clements adopted the riverboat call "mark twain" as his pen name.
to show plainly	Her smile marked her happiness.
to be ready	I am on my mark.

See how many connoted meanings you can find for the following familiar words:

term, take, tag, table, tack, sweep, snap, spread, train, and pick

Now try the simple word *run,* it has more than a dozen connoted meanings. Write your own meaning for each use as shown in the sentences that follow:

1. The boys have the *run* of the club.
   Meaning:

2. The bus *runs* past the store.
   Meaning:

3. The depression caused a *run* on the banks.
   Meaning:

4. She got a *run* in her stocking from kneeling.
   Meaning:

5. He *runs* the assembly with an iron hand.
   Meaning:

6. The dog *run* in our backyard provided exercise for our terrier.
   Meaning:

7. *The Fantasticks* had one of the longest *runs* in theatrical history.
   Meaning:

8. Reggie Jackson hit another home *run.*
   Meaning:

9. The mayor had a close *run* in the election.
   Meaning:

10. The fishermen had a *run* of good luck on trout.
    Meaning:

11. The broker *runs* up a big telephone bill.
     Meaning:

12. Anton *ran* the spear through the door.
     Meaning:

13. Cleveland *ran* for president twice.
     Meaning:

14. Pasteur *ran* down the cause of the silk-worms dying
     in Provencal.
     Meaning:

Distinctive use lifts the common and familiar out of the realm of the ordinary. Great improvement in ability to handle words can be derived by practice in replacing many overused and tired words with more pointed and graphic connotative substitutes. Read with a keen eye for finding new uses for the many words which heretofore have had only one or two meanings for you.

Meanings can be made clear by examining the use of the word in the sentence. A word may have meanings that are almost opposite, as shown by the uses of *fast* in this sentence: The torpedo was *fast* approaching its target; seconds before it had been *fast* in its tube. The first connotes great speed, and the second implies being held motionless. As with new words, new meanings must be put to work if you expect to keep them in your vocabulary.

In addition to choosing words carefully for the purpose of clarity, you must also choose clear sentence structure. Long, complex sentences can be difficult to understand because of the thicket of clauses the reader must hack his way through. Make the subjects stand out in sentences, make the modifiers clearly modify what you want them to. Avoid, however, simplistic sentences that pile upon one another lifelessly. Find a middle ground, neither too flowery nor too simple—but above all be clear.

Simplicity

Simplicity is the using of ordinary words and ordinary structures of grammar. It is not the writing of slang and common abbreviations to shorten your work. Too often, students lapse into slang when writing, without recognizing what they are doing. Some students, on the other hand, appear fond of words of many syllables and use them even when short, memorable ones are suitable. In your writing prefer simple, concrete words to vague, complex ones: *run* or *walk* instead of *move*, *group* instead of *assemblage*, *then* instead of our unfortunate heritage from the Watergate hearings, *at that point in time.*

The world knows no force sufficient to stand against the power of simple words. As the strength of a parachute is derived from each tiny thread, so is the strength of ideas dependent upon each fragile verbal tool that is used to express the idea. The strength and completeness of each oral recitation, each question you ask your teacher, each answer you write on test and examination, will depend upon how wisely you choose your words.

Half amusingly, but perhaps with more truth than can ever be known, it has been said that if Winston Churchill, in his famous speech to the British people, upon becoming prime minister in 1940, had used words such as "wounds, unrelenting labor, weeping, and perspiration," instead of the simple "blood, toil, tears, and sweat"—the British people might not have rallied to stand off Hitler until the great powers of earth could be united to destroy him.

Once you have chosen simple, direct words, use a simple grammatical structure to combine those words in sentences. Avoid piling clause upon clause—if you find yourself writing a sentence which is too long or complex, break it up into two or more shorter and simpler sentences. At the same time, do not use such a multitude of short declarative sentences that you bore your reader.

In addition to care in word choice and sentence structure, choose carefully the voice of your verbs. The most important characteristic of life is action, and speaking and writing that reflect the thoughts of life most effectively do so through action. For that reason, it is always better to use the active rather than passive voice of verbs. To say "Fishing is enjoyed by John" (passive voice), leaves John motionless; but to say "John enjoys fishing" (active voice), starts him on his way, making the subject act upon something.

After the subject, which is the reason for the thought being expressed, the *verb* is *the important word*. It carries the weight, contains the vigor, and, if carefully chosen, is capable of sound and color. Note the verbs in the sentences that follow:

1. Greece *declined* rapidly after the Battle of Mantinea in 362 B.C.; both political and cultural strength were gone.

2. Greece was *doomed* after the Battle of Mantinea in 362 B.C.; decadence, debility, and despair prevailed.

    Even though the verb *declined* is given a modifier to speed the action, it does not bring Greece crashing with the resounding sense and sound of *doom*. And what of *were gone* as compared with *prevailed*? The tense of *were gone* removes the action of political and cultural strength, but there remained action—decadence, debility, and despair *prevailed*.

Choosing Active Words

One of the glorious achievements of man, said Sophocles, was that "he has learned the use of language to express windswift thought."[5] Another translation puts it in slightly different words:

> Words also, and thought as rapid as air,
> He fashions to his good use.[6]

---

5. Sophocles, *Antigone,* trans. Agard, 143.
6. Sophocles, *Antigone,* l. 353. As translated by Dudley Fitts, *Greek Plays in Modern Translation* (New York: Dial Press, 1947), 470.

Which words impress us most when we hear or read them? Surely, those that produce action and bring a thought to life. Words, which, as Sophocles puts it, are active enough to express thoughts as swift as wind.

Sincerity

You must choose a style and words that are appropriate to the occasion. You must never be condescending, never supercilious. Your reader will know and resent your efforts.

Viewpoint is an important consideration in choosing the words you are to use. They must be selected for the person or persons to whom you wish to picture your thoughts. When Abraham Lincoln spoke at Gettysburg, he chose words, not for himself and the dignitaries who were present. He selected words that had meaning for the veterans of the battle who leaned on their crutches or dangled empty uniform sleeves in the November wind. He knew that among his listeners there would be mothers who had lost sons, wives who had lost husbands, and brothers who had lost brothers. These people would remember what he said because he spoke for them.

Churchill in his famous "Blood, Sweat, and Tears" speech did not choose his words for the members of Parliament. He chose them for the thousands of Britishers who would bleed and sweat, and bleed and sweat some more, in the impending holocaust.

There are a number of questions you should ask yourself in order to insure the point of view of the person with whom you wish to communicate: (1) What words will he clearly understand? (2) What would he really like to hear? (3) What are his interests? But far more significant, (4) What are his needs?

Having answered these questions, the point of view must be extended generally to respect the hearer's or reader's own self-respect regarding his or her abilities. Most people consider themselves capable of observing and assessing human nature, and having a capacity for imagination, broadened vision, adaptability to new ideas, and sympathetic understanding.

Order

The fourth part of style is order; logic must prevail. Think before you write. Make an outline, examine it, rearrange the parts to make the sequence of ideas logical, and then write. Write using parallelism, both in structure and in meaning. Avoid such a blunder as this:

> The football team wore white jerseys with blue numbers and gray helmets.

To create order and clarity, change the sentence by making the clauses parallel.

> The football team wore white jerseys with blue numbers and wore gray helmets.
>
> or
>
> The football team wore both gray helmets and white jerseys with blue numbers.

When you write, also keep focus in mind. Make your topic sentence clear in the paragraph, and make every sentence in the paragraph have the same subject. If you are able to write logically, with parallelism, and with focus, you will create tightly knit paragraphs.

Selection of Best Words

Diction, the name given to choice of words, demands a special concern for concreteness in words. We might have many favorite abstract words—decadence, prosperity, patience, charity, temptation. But if solid nouns and verbs can make an exact word picture, naming the subject and action of decay, or of prosperity, or of patience, then pleasant generalizations and abstractions must be passed over for the sake of clarity. The use of concrete words makes the user a firsthand dealer; abstractions make him a secondhand dealer.

Careless selection and mental laziness are the causes for vague and confusing abstractions. The stonemason would give little care to his choice of stones if he cared nothing about the pattern and the looks of his wall. The hardest part of building the wall is choosing the correct stones. Expressing your thoughts accurately is hard work, and finding the correct concrete word is the hardest part of all.

Generalization is soft, subject to misinterpretation, and sometimes popular, because it can be adapted to compromise. Concreteness is solid, totally devoid of vagueness, and graphically natural, because of its precision. Forceful or weak will be the judgment passed upon the words you use; and the essential element from which this judgment will be made is concreteness.

Concrete words need few modifiers. Care should be taken to avoid the use of overworked adjectives. If an adjective is used at all, it should be tested for efficiency: Is it the right adjective, or is there a brighter, better one? The same judgment must be made of adverbs, for nothing can muddle a word picture as quickly as "excess baggage" adverbs. If the verb is strong, the contribution of the adverb must be studied carefully before it is added. If the horse "galloped" over the pasture, to add that it galloped "rapidly" is questionable. The adverb modifying the adjective must also be studied with a critical eye. If the adjective had already put the icing on the cake, further icing or decoration might result in ostentation and gaudiness, reflecting only poor taste and contributing only to confusion. Form the habit of choosing among several synonyms to provide more exact modifiers when modifiers are necessary.

Common Usage Errors

There is a subtle distinction between acceptable oral conversation and acceptable written work. When you speak, you are present and can clarify any errors of misunderstanding by explaining further. Consequently, oral speech need not be as precise as written work. When you write, your words must bear the burden of conveying meaning all by themselves and so must be clear and follow accepted usage.

Many barbarisms have crept into written work as we have become increasingly less careful about our language. The onslaught of television, sports announcing, and advertising, because they emphasize immediacy at the expense of depth of understanding and clarity, have at least hurried if not caused the deterioration.

Most of the errors in usage arise from carelessness and lack of precision. We are content to use words without knowing clearly what they mean and without spelling them carefully. We also are content to use many words when few will suffice. Taking the time and effort to be careful with your words will improve your writing and your grades.

What follows is a selected group of common usage errors. Study them to see whether you commit any of them in your daily speech or in your written work. Then work to avoid them. In so doing, you will raise your level of understanding of your language, and you will begin to develop an ear for correct grammar and diction.

Errors of Grammar

1. Use verbal nouns (gerunds) with the possessive case rather than the participle with the objective case.

    CORRECT: I knew about *his taking* first place.
    INCORRECT: I knew about *him taking* first place.

2. Avoid using nouns as direct modifiers.

> CORRECT: an aggressive man
> INCORRECT: an aggressive-type man

To modify one noun by another, put the modifier in a prepositional phrase.

> CORRECT: an audit *of taxes by the I.R.S.*
> INCORRECT: an I.R.S. tax audit

3. Avoid using a negative with the word *hardly*.

Hardly means barely able, or not able. Thus, if you use a negative with it, you will be saying the opposite of what you mean.

To say, "The boy can't hardly climb the tree," doesn't mean that the boy is barely able to climb the tree. It means that he can climb it easily. Look at it this way: The boy cannot (hardly, not able to) climb the tree. The two negatives in a row cancel one another out.

4. Do not use the intensive pronoun as a substitute for the pronoun. Any intensive pronoun should only be used to make a noun or another pronoun stand out in the sentence.

> CORRECT: St. Paul, himself, wrote these words. (The word *himself* is intensifying the use of St. Paul.)
> CORRECT: Martha, Mary, and I went to Washington.
> INCORRECT: Martha, Mary, and myself went to Washington for the inaugural celebration. (The word *myself* has nothing to intensify.)

5. Do not use the word *that* after the word *but*.

> CORRECT: I do not doubt that Henry will become a great teacher.
> INCORRECT: I do not doubt but that Henry will become a great teacher.

CORRECT: He would have been on time, but he got stuck in traffic.

INCORRECT: He would have been on time but that he got stuck in traffic.

6.   Do not use the pronoun *they* without clearly indicating the antecedent. To use *they* in a nonspecific way is to betray fuzzy thinking; and certainly, it is not clear speaking.

INCORRECT: I want to the infirmary, and they said I had the flu.

INCORRECT: They say that the BMW is the finest car on the road today.

Who are they? The antecedents in these sentences are not expressed. No one knows who *they* are, and no one has any way of finding out.

CORRECT: I went to the infirmary, and the nurse said I had the flu.

CORRECT: All my friends say that the BMW is the finest car on the road today.

Never, never use *they* alone. Always make sure there are nouns in your sentence or paragraph to explain who *they* are.

Errors of Weakness

1.   Do not make nouns into verbs.

WEAK: The President will deplane in a half an hour.

STRONG: The President will leave the plane in half an hour.

2.   Avoid redundancies which, although correct grammatically, add nothing new to the sentence.

WEAK: He is *a man who is* too fat.

STRONG: He is too fat.

3.   Avoid tautologies, the needless repetition of ideas.

Example: reiterate again

        Reiterate means *repeat and repeat and re-*

peat some more. To use the word *again* after reiterate is to write a tautology.

Example: *I don't like it, myself.*

Myself adds nothing to this sentence, nor does it, because of its late position in the sentence, intensify the pronoun **I**.

Example: *true facts*

Facts can only be true, otherwise they are not facts at all.

Example: *In my mind I think Pete Rose is a great baseball player.*

Pray tell, where else does one think?

4.   Do not modify the word *unique.*

Unique means "singular, one of a kind." So to say that someone is *very unique* is to say that he or she is "very one-of-a-kind." How can anyone be "very one," or "more one," or "less one?" One can only be one. Use *unique* without any modifier.

Misuse of Words

1.   can, may

can means "be able to."

Example: He can climb the mountain.

May means "be permitted to."

Example: He may keep the book if he likes it.

2.   disinterested, uninterested

Disinterested means "impartial."

Example: Lawyers strive to find disinterested jurors.

Uninterested means "lacking in interest."

Example: Television commercials try to persuade uninterested viewers to buy new cars.

3.   effect, affect

The prefixes give the clue here. *Ef* means "from," *af* means "toward"; so *effect* describes something that comes out of a situation, and *affect* describes something that comes to a situation.

Effect, as a noun, is the result (what came out) of an action; and as a verb, it means to produce the result.

Example: The elements of careful design combined for a stunning effect when the curtain rose on the first act.

Affect is a verb meaning to influence.

Example: How did your training affect your playing?

4.   Farther, further
Both declare that something has advanced. Nonetheless, they are not interchangeable.

   a.   *Farther* is used for distance in air, on land, or at sea.

   Example: The sloop is farther out in the bay than the launch.

   b.   *Further* is used for distance in time.

   Example: The scientist engaged in further study.

5.   Imply, infer
Imply means "to express indirectly."

   Example: The reporter implied that the mayor was corrupt.

   Infer means "to draw a conclusion."

   Example: What can you infer from her choice of words?

6.   like, as
These two words are misused more often than any others. Never use them interchangeably. To keep them straight, remember how they are used.

   a.   *Like* will modify nouns and is never used in verbal expressions. It means "similar to."
   Example: She is like my sister.

   b.   *As* is a conjunction or adverb and should be used with verbs or phrases. It means, when used as an adverb, "equally," "when," or "where."
   Example: He is as tall as my brother.

When used as a conjunction the word *as* means "because," "since."

Example: As you are going to town anyway, will you post this letter for me?

7. less, fewer
Both declare that something has been reduced in quantity. Nonetheless, they should not be used interchangeably.
a. *Less* should only be used with abstractions.

Example: Because of my illness, I have less time to complete my research paper.

b. *Fewer* should only be used with numbers of concrete nouns.

Example: This flock has fewer sheep than that flock.

8. Loan, lend
a. *Loan* is a noun.

Example: One goes to a bank to seek a loan.

b. *Lend* is a verb.

Examples: It is improper to say, "Please loan me some money."
It is proper to say, "Please lend me some money."

9. There, their
a. *There* is an adverb or is an expletive.

Examples: (*adverb*) Look over there.
(*expletive*) There are many errors of usage.

b. *Their* is a possessive.

Example: The boys said that their brother had won the bicycle race.

10. *Transpire* is used incorrectly as a substitute for *occurred*. Means to "become known," not "to happen."

INCORRECT: The lawyer asked the witness what had transpired.

CORRECT: The lawyer asked the witness what had occurred.

11. Two, to, too
    a. *Two* is a number.

    Example: There are two books on the table.

    b. *To* is a preposition or a particle indicating an infinitive.

    Examples: (*preposition*) Mary ran to the car.
    (*particle*) It is difficult to run twenty-six miles without stopping.

    c. *Too* is an adverb.

    Example: The boy was too large to sit on the high chair.

Misuse of Prepositions

1. Avoid the phrase *kind of* when you mean "rather."

    INCORRECT: She was kind of pretty.
    CORRECT: She was rather pretty.

2. Remember that *of* is a preposition, while *have* is a verb.

    INCORRECT: He would *of* been on time, had he started earlier.
    CORRECT: He would *have* been on time, had he started earlier.

3. *Due to* has come to mean "because" rather than an expression to indicate something owed. When you mean to say *because*, say so, by using *because*.

    Examples: Homage is due a king.
    The steeplechase was cancelled because the track was muddy.

4. *Inside of*—do not use *of*. *Inside* is complete by itself.

5. *Later on*—do not use *on*. *Later* is complete by itself.

6. *Off of*—do not use *of*. *Off* is complete by itself.

7. *Plan on*—do not use *on*. *Plan* is complete by itself.

8. *Subsequent to*—why use two words when one will do? When you mean *after*, use the word itself; say *after*, not *subsequent to*.

9. *Prior to*—again, why use two words? When you mean *before*, say so; use *before*, do not use *prior to*.

10. *Words with prefixes*. When using words that have prefixes, use the English preposition that has a meaning similar to the prefix.
    According to (*ac* = to) is much more concise than "in accordance with" and so is preferable.

11. different than, different from
    Different from (*dif* = from) is the only proper construction. *Different than* is simply wrong; "than" is not a preposition; it is used to indicate the second of two parts in a comparison and must follow an adjective in the comparative degree.
    Examples: Suzy is different from Cathy.
    Suzy is taller than Cathy. (Note the adjective in the comparative degree, *taller*, and that Cathy is the second of two parts of a comparison.)

Barbarisms

Barbarisms are those words that have crept into our language and insidiously eaten away at clarity and forceful speech. Excise them from your everyday language and from your prose.

1. Irregardless
    Irregardless is a redundancy that betrays incompetence in language and lack of care.
    Regardless means "without concern." Adding the prefix *ir*, which means "not" or "without," makes the word mean "not without concern,"—the opposite of what you are trying to say.

2. Enthuse

Enthuse is a verb that has sprung from a noun. Such creation of verbs is weak and ultimately shows that the speaker lacks precision.

Do not say: Edith was enthused about her recent trip to Europe.

Say instead: Edith was pleased, or Edith was happy, or Edith was enthusiastic, about her trip.

3. -ize or -ness words

Avoid turning words into nouns by adding the suffixes *-ize* or *-ness*.

Examples: (*-ness*) These suffixes betray a lack of specificness in language.

(*-ize*) Finalize your plans, at this point in time, to rid yourself vocabularywise of such barbarisms.

Almost any word that contains these suffixes can be replaced by a much stronger word.

Do not use *prioritize*, use instead *assign priorities*.
Do not use *finalize*, use instead *finish*.
Do not use *humbleness*, use instead *humility*.
Do not use *speediness*, use instead *speed*.

4. -wise words

Also avoid turning adjectives into adverbs by adding the suffix *-wise*. In general, you can better express your idea by a prepositional phrase.

Do not use *contrarywise*, use instead *on the contrary*.
Do not use *likewise*, use instead *in a similar way*.

Looking Back

1. The primary elements of a good writing style are emphasized in this chapter. The first one is obvious: *clarity*. What are the other three that were mentioned?

Of the four qualities, which one could you neglect and still be considered a good writer?

2. Explain the difference between *denotation* and *connotation*. Give examples in support of your explanation.

How many connoted meanings can you list for *light, free, head*?

Look back at the fourteen different sentences that contain some form of *run*. Do the same for the word *sink*.

3. Which of the following sentences is correct?
    a. Sylvia can't hardly play the piano.
    b. I would of passed the test if I had been present.
    c. We returned back to the beach after lunch.
    d. How will the election affect the stock market?
    e. Alyse has less subjects than her twin sister, Gail.
    If any sentences are wrong, how would you correct them?

14

RESEARCH PAPERS: STEPS TO SUCCESS

True Confessions

1. You are asked to do a term paper (minimum of seven thousand words) for your English class on some phase of Shakespeare's life or his works. Does the assignment send chills down your spine? How will you proceed to select your topic, to begin the research?

2. The assignment for the research paper on Shakespeare is given to you the third week in September. The paper, suitably typewritten, with footnotes and bibliography, is due the first week in December. What kind of schedule would you prepare to enable you to get the work done on time?

3. Here are two footnotes from a page in a library book; can you explain all that they contain?

   1. George Fischer, *Shakespeare's Education* (Bellmore, New York: Ellis & Sloane, 1972), 71.
   2. Ibid., 75.

What is a Research Paper?

A research paper is an opportunity for you to show several things: (1) that you can examine a topic in detail, (2) that you know research methods, (3) that you know your way around a library, (4) that you can organize a bulk of information in a proper way, and (5) that you can write clearly. So remember that a research paper is an opportunity to show how good a student you are. Do not approach the task of writing one as a terrible burden, a task to be avoided as long as possible.

When you are doing a research paper, you will be reading books and articles written by others about your topic. You will be tempted to use their knowledge as if it were your own. If you do, you may be guilty of plagiarism.

Plagiarism is the taking of someone else's words or ideas and presenting them as your own. Thus, plagiarism is fundamentally dishonest, it is a kind of thievery. Students who are idea-thieves are going on record as cheaters who cannot think for themselves and will receive the low grade they deserve.

It is inevitable, however, that you will use the ideas that others have thought about your topic. The way to do so honestly, avoiding plagiarism, is to tell your readers who created the ideas you are using. The way to tell your readers is to write footnotes or endnotes giving the name of the work and author whose ideas you have used. Later in this chapter you will find information about the form such notes should take.

The Nine Steps in Research

Like other jobs you do as a student, the task of writing a research paper can be broken down into sequential steps. There are nine steps in research.

1. The first is to read in general literature in the subject area you choose to examine. It may seem strange to begin reading before you have chosen a topic, but you will find that by reading in general literature, you will

be able to choose a specific topic that interests you and for which there is sufficient information to do a paper.

In order to read in general literature, you must have an idea about your topic. For example, if you have received an assignment in history to write a paper on something that happened in the years from 1609 to 1865, you should think about what era you want to examine. Would it be the Puritans, the Revolution, the War of 1812, or the Writing of the Constitution? Then, once you have chosen the general area, you would go to the reference section of your library and read articles in the encyclopedias and specialized reference works dealing with U. S. history, such as *Dictionary of American Biography*. You could also read sections of a standard textbook of U. S. history.

2. As you do your reading in general literature, you should be looking for a suitable topic. Finding your topic is the second step in writing a paper.

    After you have chosen your topic, limit it. Think about what particular aspect of it you are going to examine. For example, if you decided to do research on the writing of the U. S. Constitution, you could limit your topic to "the role of James Madison in the writing of the Constitution," or "the seventeenth century political philosophers who influenced the writers of the Constitution" or perhaps "the role of Benjamin Franklin in the writing of the Constitution." By limiting your topic, you are making it specific. You will be able to guide your research and avoid reading works that pertain to your general area of research, but not to your specific topic. This limiting of your topic will become a great time saver.

3. The next step in the process of writing a research paper is to write a working outline. A working outline is a preliminary organizer for your research. You will make your thesis statement, saying what it is that you will try to prove, and then divide your topic into its natural,

general divisions. You will not need to make this outline detailed—merely a statement of what the major areas of the topic are. For example, to continue, let's see what a preliminary outline might be for the topic, "The role of James Madison in writing the Constitution."

I.   Thesis statement: Madison the "architect" of our Constitution

II. Early Life
     A. Childhood, adolescence, things Madison studied
     B. What Madison did during the Revolution

III. How the Constitution was written
     A. Nature of government under "Articles of Confederation"; failure of that government
     B. Convening of the Constitutional Convention
     C. How the convention operated
         1. Factions
             a. Supporters of "Articles"
             b. "Federalists"
         2. Major ideas that were proposed

IV. Role of Madison
     A. His faction
     B. Importance to that faction
     C. His accomplishments
         1. When Convention opened
         2. As the Federalists' proposals came forth
     D. Madison's proposals

V.   Final form of Constitution.
     A. Brief survey of theoretical model of U. S. Government
     B. Madison's contribution

VI. Conclusion showing that thesis statement is proved

4. The fourth step in doing a research paper is to write bibliography cards of the books and articles you will read. Use 3 × 5 cards, one book or article per card.

    To find the names of the books, use all the resources of the reference room of the library. Encyclopedia articles will recommend books to read for further study; indexes, such as the *Readers Guide to Periodical Literature*, will provide help. Use the card catalogue of the books in the library. Ask the reference librarians for help; they are a resource, too!

    When you have found a likely book or article, put down all the publisher's information on your card. For a book, put the full name of the author, the full title (including subtitle), the name of the publisher, the place of publication, and the copyright date. For articles, write the name of the author (if given), title of the article (if given), the name of the magazine or encyclopedia, the date of issue of the particular magazine or encyclopedia, the page numbers of the article. If you are reading an encyclopedia article, include all the publishing information that you would include for any book. These bibliography cards will contain all the information you need when writing footnotes or bibliographies.

5. The fifth step is to read the works and take notes. Take your notes on 5 × 8 or 4 × 6 cards, one note to a card. Write only on one side of the card. If your note runs over one card, write on a second card rather than on the back of the first card. That way, when you lay the cards on your desk as you write, you won't have to turn them over to see what is on the back, and you will save time.

    At the top of each card write an abbreviation of the title of the work cited and the pages in the work from which the note came. Write down direct quotations if you must, but it is better to put the notes in your own words. Keep your cards in a box or packet—don't lose them.

6. After you have taken your notes, write a detailed outline of your paper. This outline is the one from which

you will write your paper, so make it as detailed as you can. Make the arrangement of your ideas clear and logical.

7. Then assemble your note cards, putting them in the order of your final outline, and begin to write your first draft.

8. After your rough draft, revise and revise again, until you are satisfied with your paper.

9. Finally, put your paper in the form required by your teacher, using acceptable footnote and bibliography formats.

Proceeding to Do Research

The first thing you should do when assigned a research paper is to write down a schedule. Allot time to each of the nine steps, allowing about ⅓ of the total time for Steps 1–4, about ⅓ for reading and taking notes, and the remaining third for composing the paper, Steps 6–9.

To allot time to the steps, start your estimates from the date the paper is due and work backwards. For example, you have received an assignment from your history teacher and have been told that the research paper must be turned in on the last day of the term, nine weeks later.

Write a schedule like the one below, and put the date the paper is due next to Step 9. Then, next to Step 5, put the date of the day that is three weeks before the end of the term. Then, next to Step 4, put the date of the day that is six weeks before the end of the term.

After you have divided the available time into the major parts, subdivide the major areas. In our example you were given nine weeks to complete the assignment. Your division would be something like this: Of the three weeks for Steps 1–4, allow yourself about five days for general reading, about two days for selecting and limiting your topic, and about two weeks for collecting your working bibliography; of the three weeks you allow yourself for writing, estimate that your outline will take five days, composing the rough draft about five days, revising about six days, and preparing the final copy about five days.

Date Due	Step Number	Description of Step	Check Mark to Show Step Done
	1	Read in general lit.	
	2	Select & limit topic	
	3	Write a working outline	
	4	Collect working bibliography	
	5	Read and take notes	
	6	Write detailed outline	
	7	Write rough draft	
	8	Revise, revise, and revise	
	9	Put final draft in required form	

Once your schedule is in place, you are ready to begin. As you search through general literature, be systematic in your efforts. Being systematic is perhaps the key to success in doing research. Look carefully at all available general literature, and then when you begin to collect your bibliography, be systematic in the writing of the cards. When you are writing your notes, be systematic again. Make sure every notation is *clear*, especially the page numbers, so that you will not have to retrace your steps and redo some research because you couldn't remember from which source a good idea came.

Footnotes and Bibliography

You must give the source for every idea and quotation you use in your paper. Otherwise you are being academically dishonest.

Give the sources for the ideas you use in proper footnote or endnote form. Footnotes and endnotes follow the same form. However, they appear in different places in your paper. As the names suggest, footnotes are put at the foot of the page on which the citation occurs, and endnotes at the end of the paper. Use whichever type your teacher prefers.

Footnotes and endnotes must contain:

For a book
1. Author's complete name, first name first
2. Title of work, underlined
3. Editor, compiler, or translator, if there is one
4. Series, if any; volume in the series
5. Edition number, if book is not the first edition
6. Number of volumes, if there are more than one
7. Publication facts, in parentheses:
   city of publisher
   publisher
   publication date
8. Volume number, if there is more than one volume
9. Number of page on which the idea or quotation appears

For an article
1. Author's name, if given
2. Article title, in quotation marks
3. Title of magazine, journal, or book (underlined) in
   which article appears

4. Volume number and issue number of magazine or jour-
    nal—if a book, give date of publication, including
    all publishing information (as asked for above)
5. Number of page on which idea or quotation appears

Here are two footnote examples:

For a book
   John J. Audubon, *Birds of America* (New York: Macmillan,
   1946), 14.
For a magazine
   Allan Devoe, "Our Feathered Friends," *Nature Magazine*
   21 (October 1951): 21–23.

It is likely that you will want to cite the same work a number
of times in the course of your paper. It would be awkward and
time-consuming to write out the full citation each time. To save
yourself time and effort, you may use shortened references. The
first time a reference to a book or an article appears it must be
given in full; however, subsequent references may appear in
shortened form.

There are two methods of shortening references. One involves
giving the last name of the author, a shortened version of the
book or article title, and the appropriate page number. For example:

1. Albert Einstein, *The World As I See It* (Princeton Uni-
    versity Press, 1949), 84.
2. Einstein, *The World*, 104.

The second method involves omitting the book or article title
and giving only the author's last name followed by a comma and
the appropriate page reference.

You should be aware that some scholars still use certain abbreviations to shorten footnote and bibliography references, but
this practice has fallen out of use to a great degree. The following
list is given only to make you aware of these abbreviations. The

three most frequently used are: *ibid.* (Latin, meaning the same place), *op. cit.* (Latin, meaning the work cited or quoted), and *loc. cit.* (Latin, meaning in the place cited).

anon.—anonymous
c. or ca.—circa (about)
cf.—compare or confer
ch., chaps.—chapter, chapters
col., cols.—column, columns
e.g.—exempli gratia (for example)
et. seq.—et sequens (and following)
f., ff.—following page, following pages
fac.—facsimile
fig., figs.—figure, figures
l, ll—line, lines
id, idem.—in the same place
i.e.—id est (that is)
ms., mss.—manuscript, manuscripts
n.—note
n.b.—nota bene (note well)
n.d.—no date
no., nos.—number, numbers
n.p.—no publisher
n.s.—new series
p., pp.—page, pages
pseud.—pseudonym
sec., secs.—section, sections
sic—thus
[sic]—error recopied from original
v.—verse
viz.—namely
vol., vols.—volume, volumes

Footnotes, like a sound bibliography, make your paper more scholarly and interesting. It is better to use too many than too few, but they can be overdone. Use them to reflect your honesty in recognizing the important sources from which you have gathered information and to add interest to your theme. Observe one or two of your textbooks or several scholarly books in your school library for effective models of footnotes and bibliographies.

At the end of your paper you will write a list of the books you used. This list is called the bibliography. There are two kinds of bibliographies: one contains only those works from which you quoted or got ideas (all properly footnoted, of course), and the other contains those works that you consulted. This latter type includes all the works you cited and also other works that pertain to your topic, but which you did not use as sources. Make sure to ask your teacher which kind of bibliography is required for your paper.

Again, as in footnoting, a proper format is necessary. You must include all information necessary for someone else to be able to find the book or magazine in a library. The form of the bibliography entry is different, slightly, from the footnote entry.

For a book
1. Author's complete name, last name first, followed by a period.
2. Title of work, underlined, followed by a period.
3. Editor, compiler, or translator, if there is one, followed by a period.
4. Edition, if not the first, followed by a period.
5. Number of volumes, if more than one, followed by a period.
6. Publication facts:
    city of publisher, followed by a colon
    publisher, followed by a comma
    publication date, followed by a period.

For an article
1. Author's name, last name first, followed by a period.
2. Article title, in quotation marks, followed by a period.
3. Publication facts:
    Name of magazine, journal, or book, underlined, but not followed by any mark of punctuation
    Volume number of magazine or journal
    Publication date, in parentheses, followed by a colon.
4. Page numbers, inclusive, of the article, followed by a period.

Below are two examples of bibliography entries.

Audubon, John J. *Birds of America*. New York: Macmillan, 1946.

Devoe, Allan. "Our Feathered Friends." *Nature Magazine* 21 (October 1951): 21–23.

Usually bibliographies are divided into sections, books first and then articles. Sometimes they are divided into sections for primary sources (eyewitness accounts) and secondary sources (people writing about something that they themselves did not witness). In each section of the bibliography the entries are alphabetical, according to the last name of the author, or if the author's name is not given, according to the first word of the title.

A Word of Caution

The term paper or research theme, if approached by the student as a difficult and time-consuming burden, usually turns out a boring and padded piece of work that boldly betrays the writer's lack of interest. If the theme is looked upon as a challenge and a chance for discovery and creative work, the product is what one would expect—a well written essay, reflecting wide reading and grasp of material, and intellectually stimulating to the teacher who reads it.

Originality in the term paper is always of great value, but your grade probably is derived more from the scope of the paper—scope referring to the extent of the writer's reading on the subject before he or she starts to write. Originality, like all other inventiveness, is not the gift of all, but there is no student who cannot read widely and fulfill the basic obligation of having a good working knowledge of the subject. Only by doing the extensive study first, does the writer ever arrive at the place where the imaginative consideration of the ideas of others may bring into existence new ideas. Usually a new idea is born from combining ideas from other sources, so the student who deludes himself by thinking that he can write a successful paper without extensive background reading will doubtless be rudely disillusioned by a poor grade.

Practices for Better Research Papers

1. Make a schedule of the nine steps in research and assign a date for completion of each step. Put the schedule in your work place.
2. Allow ⅓ of your allotted time for writing.
3. Use all of the resources of your library, including the librarian.
4. If you find you have chosen a topic for which you can't gain ready access to information, *change your topic*, and revise your work schedule. You should be able to tell whether you need to change when you try to compile your working bibliography. If you can't find many books and articles, take the hint—you will have a difficult time gathering notes and writing your paper.
5. Be systematic in taking your notes. Make sure that every page number is accurate and that you will be able to find the passage cited if you are asked to do so.

Looking Back

1. Why is it important for a footnote to contain the publication date of a book? Why the place of publication?
   CLUES: Suppose it were a book on physics or one on economics.

2. "The nine research steps are very comprehensive," said Josh, "but as I see it, unless you pick the right topic, you are in deep trouble."

    What's your reaction to Josh's statement? Is selection of the right topic the most important of all the steps? Why?

3. Let us suppose that you selected "Shakespeare and Religion" as your topic. You scour the public library and your school's library, but find only two brief references to the topic. *The Encyclopedia Britannica* provides you with a few additional notes.

    You have four weeks left to complete and submit the research paper. What should you do?

15

THE LIBRARY: HOW TO USE IT

True Confessions

ı. In your opinion, what is the most important room in your school? In your town?

The first paragraph of this chapter suggests that the library is the most important room in both schools and towns. Tell why you agree or disagree.

2. Time for a true or false test:
   a. The Dewey Decimal System is especially useful for those taking algebra tests. T or F?
   b. Roget's *Thesaurus* is a beautiful sculpture of an extinct animal. T or F?
   c. *The Reader's Guide* recommends worthwhile books for high-school and college students. T or F?

   Can you explain why the answer is F to all three questions?

3. Today's libraries contain much more than books. Name at least three other kinds of materials you are likely to find there.

How to Find a Book

In Chapter 4 it was suggested that your libraries provide both atmosphere and incentive for serious study, and that if you do not have satisfactory conditions at home, the library habit could become one of your best study habits. The most important room or building at your school and in your town or city is perhaps the library. It is the purpose of this chapter to prepare you to find what you want in the library and make known to you what is available there.

Knowing the parts of a book—title, author, publisher, date of publication, edition—is the first step toward finding what you want in the library. With this information you are prepared to enter and find whether or not the book you want is in the library. For this you go to the card catalogue.

The card catalogue is not a catalogue in book form. It is rather a series of drawers labeled with letters of the alphabet. The card files are really an alphabetical index to the library. All cards are filed alphabetically, beginning with the first important word of the title—*A, An,* and *The* are omitted. In addition to the title card there are also author and subject cards. The title card is the quickest if you know what book you want.

EXAMPLE OF TITLE CARD:

	Audubon bird guide.
	Pough, Richard G.
598.2	Audubon bird guide; eastern land birds.
P	Doubleday, 1946.

Suppose you read the book and decide that you would like to read some more of the author's works. You return the book you have read to the library and check the *author card* for additional books. There will be an author card for each separate work of the author. As an example, let us imagine you have read John Kieran's *An Introduction to Birds* and are checking the author cards for more books by him. On the author card his name will be listed *Kieran, John.* If the library has his *Birds of New York City,* it will be first. The next author card will probably list *Footnotes on Nature*; and the third, arranged alphabetically, will be the book you have just returned, *Introduction to Birds,* with the article *An* omitted. The author card usually gives the most complete information regarding the book, but it may contain the same facts as the other cards.

EXAMPLE OF AUTHOR CARD:

598.2   Pough, Richard H.
P   Audubon bird guide; eastern land birds.
            Doubleday, 1946.
            Birds
            t.

Suppose you wish to pursue your study of birds, but do not know authors or titles. A third card is available to help you. It is called the *subject card,* and may be indexed as a general subject (BIRDS) or as a specific subject (SONG BIRDS). Subject cards are either printed with the subject in capitals or in red ink to distinguish them.

EXAMPLE OF SUBJECT CARD:

            BIRDS
598.2   Pough, Richard H.
P   Audubon bird guide; eastern land birds.
            Doubleday, 1946.

SUBJECT CARD (MORE COMPLETE)

            AMERICAN FOLKWAYS
917.63   Kane, Harnett Thomas 1910–
K   Deep Delta Country, Duell, 1944.
            XX, 283 p. maps. Selected bibliography
            pp. 273–80.

Subject cards are not included for fiction except for historical novels of recognized merit.

You cannot carry the file to show the librarian what you want. You must write out (sometimes special forms are provided) the following information: (1) call number, (2) author's name, (3) title, (4) volume and edition, and (5) your own name.

You have probably been wondering what all the numbers on the cards are for. The numbers are symbols in a classification system, providing you with a call number by which you request the book. The same number tells the librarian in what section of the library, on what shelf, and in what specific place on the shelf the book is to be found.

Systems of Classification

There are two widely used systems of classification: the Dewey Decimal System and the Library of Congress System. The Dewey Decimal system is the one you will probably use most often. It was developed at Amherst College in 1873 and catalogues all knowledge under *ten divisions,* each division being assigned a group of numbers.

DEWEY DECIMAL SYSTEM

NUMBERS	MAIN DIVISIONS	SUBDIVISIONS
000-099	General Works	Almanacs, encyclopedias, bibliographies, magazines, newspapers. Materials that cannot be narrowed to a single subject.
100-199	Philosophy	Logic, history of philosophy, systems of philosophy, ethics, and psychology.
200-299	Religion	Sacred writings (the Bible), mythology, history of religions, all religions and theologies.
300-399	Sociology (Social Sciences)	Group dynamics, law, government, education, economics.
400-499	Philology (Study of Lingustics)	Dictionaries dealing with words (not of biographies), grammars

DEWEY DECIMAL SYSTEM (*Continued*)

NUMBERS	MAIN DIVISIONS	SUBDIVISIONS
		and technical studies of all languages.
500-599	Science (Subject and Theoretical)	Astronomy, biology, botany, chemistry, mathematics, physics, etc.
600-699	Applied Science (Useful Arts)	Agriculture, all types of engineering, business, home economics, medicine, nursing, etc.
700-799	Fine Arts (Professional and Recreative)	Architecture, painting, music, performing arts, sports, etc.
800-899	Literature	All types of literature—drama, essays, novels, poetry, etc.—in all languages of all countries.
900-999	History	All history, biography, geography, and travel, etc.

If you go to the section of the library shelving Applied Science, 600-699, you will see immediately that each division is further divided. For example, 600-610 will have general books or collections dealing with applied science. Medicine will be classified under 610. Books on engineering will begin with 520 and be further broken down by smaller decimals. A glance at the history shelves will reveal that 900-909 are general works of history; 910 is geography; and so on by decimal subdivision. English is subdivided into literature of nations, then further catalogued. For example, English literature is 820; English poetry 821; English drama 822; and so on to 829.99. English poetry, 821, is further subdivided; 821.1 is Early English poetry; and so on to 821.9, each subdivision designating a specific period. A little observation will make it easy for you to find the exact spot in a particular section of the library where the subject you are interested in can be pinpointed.

The Library of Congress system of classification designates the main divisions of knowledge by letters instead of numbers. Subdivisions in the Library of Congress System are made by the addition of a second letter and whole numbers. No detailed explanation will be given of this system beyond the letter classification of knowledge.

LIBRARY OF CONGRESS SYSTEM

LETTER	MAIN DIVISIONS
A	General Works
B	Philosophy and Religion
C	History—Auxiliary Sciences
D	History—Topography (except American)
E–F	American History—Topography
G	Geography—Anthropology
H	Social Sciences
J	Political Sciences
K	Law
L	Education
M	Music
N	Fine Arts
P	Language—Literature (nonfiction)
Q	Sciences
R	Medicine
S	Agriculture
T	Technology
U	Military Science
V	Naval Science
Z	Bibliography and Library Science
P–Z	Literature (fiction)

Fiction and Biography

Fiction and biography are usually arranged in a section set aside for each, and the cataloguing is usually simplified. This is always true of fiction. In the fiction section, the books are arranged alphabetically by the author's last name. In case of two or more books by the same author, they are shelved alphabetically by title. Some libraries use the classification symbol *F* or *Fic* plus the first letter of the author's last name.

Biography is usually classified by the letter *B* or the number *92*. However, some libraries classify individual biographies under *921* and collective biographies under *920*. The *B* and *92* classifications also carry the first letter of the last name of the person written about. Thus, a biography of Abraham Lincoln would be designated B or 92. Biographies are arranged on the
                    L   L
shelf alphabetically by the last name of the person written about. In case of more than one biography written about the same man, arrangement is alphabetically by author name. Collective biographies are arranged alphabetically according to the author or compiler's name.

Here is a card for colective biography. Some of the information is explained below:

①
920   Rome—Biography
P   Plutarch
                   Plutarch's Lives. The translation
                   called Dryden's. Corrected from Greek
                   and revised by A. H. Clough—
          ②   5 v. Boston, Little, Brown and Co. 1872
          ③   L.C. DE7. P5 1872   ④   8—14601

① Call number
② Five volumes
③ Library of Congress Catalogue number
④ Copyright number

With this information fresh in your mind, visit your school or public library. Discover the ease with which you can find your way from one section to another, and remember it, so you will not have to roam. Wandering from section to section and from shelf to shelf each time you visit the library wastes your time and is probably annoying to people who are trying to concentrate on their work.

Reference Books

Reference books provide invaluable help to the student by making important information easily accessible. That is the whole function of the reference section of the library. As you prepare themes, reports, essays, or research papers, you can help yourself get a good start by using these books. They not only will give you general information about a topic, but will direct you to other works that cover your topic in greater depth.

Reference sections of libraries will contain many different kinds of works, and what follows here is merely a guide to some basic kinds of reference books.

Perhaps the first book to catch your eye in the reference section of the library will be an unabridged dictionary, a book of such size that it has its own special rack. An unabridged dictionary contains nearly all the words in the language, giving definitions, showing pronunciation, and presenting information about the origin and history of each word. As well as entries about words, such a dictionary contains biographical and geographical information, abbreviations, tables of weights and measures, and commonly used foreign phrases. Two unabridged dictionaries often found are Merriam-Webster's unabridged dictionary and the Random House unabridged dictionary of the English language. The most comprehensive of all the dictionaries is the *Oxford English Dictionary*. It is many volumes long, and because of the exhaustive length and the high quality of its scholarship, it is the most respected authority on words.

In order to use these massive books, you will need to know the abbreviations the editors have used. Abbreviations and their meanings will be listed, either in the front or back. Be sure to consult this list whenever you are in doubt about the meaning of an entry.

In addition to dictionaries, reference sections of libraries may contain thesauruses of words, usually Roget's or a modernized version of this work. A thesaurus is a compilation of synonyms and so is valuable to anyone doing any kind of writing.

Another source of good information about words is *The New Century Cyclopedia of Names,* which provides an abundance of information about the origins, history, and meaning of names used in English. Two sources of information about English as spoken and written in the United States are H. L. Mencken's *The American Language* and Bergen Evans' *Dictionary of Contemporary American Usage.*

In your English class you may be asked to write essays about works of literature. The reference section of the library contains many examples of literary criticism and much information about authors. *Contemporary Literary Criticism* is a collection of reviews of books by living authors. *Twentieth Century Literary Criticism* contains biographical essays about authors, as well as collections of reviews and essays about them. *Contemporary Authors* has few reviews of works, but is filled with biographical information about living authors, including lists of titles of their written works. *Book Review Digest* is perhaps the standard reference of literary criticism, for it contains excerpts from reviews of almost all published nonfiction and fiction. Any work of nonfiction that receives two reviews in periodicals or journals will be listed and so will any work of fiction that receives four reviews.

Whenever you are asked to do a research paper, one place to look for a topic is in general encyclopedias. Encyclopedias, their very name derived from the Greek *enkyklios* ("encircle") and *paideia* ("education"), enclose in one volume or set of volumes masses of information on nearly any conceivable topic.

Every reference section of libraries will contain encyclopedias, some libraries will have several. Most common are *World Book,* especially written for younger people, *Americana, Britannica,* and *Colliers,* but there are others as well. Most encyclopedias update their information by adding a volume, called an annual or a yearbook, each year for a decade or so after publication.

All encyclopedias are arranged alphabetically by subject, and most contain indexes both to topics and contributing authors. The essays in encyclopedias are written by experts; give information in a clear, compact form; and will often contain a brief bibliography of other works that pertain to the essay's topic.

In addition to these encyclopedias of many volumes, there is an excellent single volume work, *The Columbia Encyclopedia*. It covers the vast array of human knowledge, but necessarily devotes less space to topics than a multiple-volumed work does.

There are also specialized encyclopedias that deal with particular subjects and are limited to particular fields of knowledge such as art, science, technology, music, or history. Libraries sometimes have encyclopedias that limit their scope to particular religions and ethnic groups, such as the *Catholic Encyclopedia* or the *Jewish Encyclopedia*.

For information on contemporary events you can turn to one or another of the yearbooks that you might find in the reference section. *Facts on File* is an annual collection of digests of news articles on current events, and all subjects are indexed for easy use. Annuals, such as the *World Almanac*, contain up-to-date statistics, some valuable facts about government agencies and personnel, sports, scientific developments, and information on many other topics. Both national and state governments produce yearbooks of various kinds. You will find all of these works to be of great assistance if you have to prepare a paper on contemporary developments.

Most reference sections also contain numerous biographical dictionaries. Some volumes will be specifically devoted, for example, to musicians, writers, or statesmen. Others will give sketches of noteworthy persons from every walk of life. *Who's Who in America, Dictionary of American Biography, Webster's Biographical Dictionary,* and *Chambers's Biographical Dictionary* are general works. *Dictionary of National Biography* is devoted to noteworthy citizens of Great Britain. *Current Biography,* published in magazine form several times a year, and put in book form by years, is a place to gather facts on someone who has become prominent in the immediate present.

In addition to contemporary material afforded by yearbooks, there are many interesting and valuable articles in magazines and newspapers. *The Reader's Guide to Periodical Literature* is the standard reference to magazine articles. The *Reader's Guide* is published twice a month and lists alphabetically, by author, subject, and title, the significant articles from more than a hundred magazines. *The New York Times Index* is a guide to the articles found in that newspaper. The *Index* is published monthly and lists alphabetically, by subject, articles and editorials that appeared in the newspaper.

Records and Films

Many school and public libraries have good audiovisual departments, containing recordings of famous speeches, color slides of paintings, architectural illustrations, and other pictures relating to geography, history, and all other aspects of knowledge. Ask the librarians for help in unlocking their treasure chest of visual materials.

Recent advances in photography have made a great deal of material available to libraries through microfilms and microcards. Vast quantities of information have been reduced in volume and in cost by these techniques, and so many libraries have been able to expand their holdings. Most microfilm or microcard holdings will be of newspapers, periodicals, or rare books. As you do research for history papers or perhaps for an English paper, you may find the articles you want to read are on film. Ask your librarian for help in finding the articles you want and in using the microfilm reading machine.

It was stated at the beginning of this chapter that the most important room or building at your school or in your town may be the library. There is no better way to end this chapter than simply to state that tests given to both high-school and college students reveal that those who make the highest marks are those who know how to use the library and do use it. It is the place most conducive to study, the place that provides the greatest storehouse of material from which to learn; so learn to use it, and use it to boost your marks, widen your horizons, and enlarge your life.

Practices for Better Library Use

1. Form the library habit. It is a place for quiet study and exciting discovery.

2. Learn the meaning of "call number" and the use of *author, title,* and *subject* catalogue cards.

3. Know the Dewey Decimal system and the location of the several divisions in your school or public library.

4. Know the methods of arranging fiction and biography used by your library. Arrangements vary from one library to another.

5. Study the reference section to learn generally what is available, its location, and the use to which the various materials may be put.

6. Learn to make a working bibliography as you find material on the topic you are studying. For a model bibliography, check several at the end of articles in one or two encyclopedias. Use the card method (3 × 5 index cards) of making your bibliography so you can rearrange at will. Know the difference between a working and an exhaustive bibliography (an exhaustive bibliography lists everything ever written on the topic). Choose a limited topic, some significant yet not too well-known historical character, and discover the excitement and methodical investigation involved in preparing a complete bibliography. Be sure to limit your topic—not *Financiers of the American Revolution,*

rather *Haym Salomon*—not the *Mimic* (Mimidae) *Family* of birds, rather the *Mockingbird*.

Looking Back

1. Using the Dewey Decimal System, where would you look to find the following books?
    a. *Concepts in Modern Biology* by David Kraus
    b. *The Essential Shakespeare* by John Dover Wilson
    c. *Economics* by Paul A. Samuelson

2. What kind of information can we expect to find about words in the *Merriam Webster Unabridged Dictionary*?
    Use that dictionary or any other unabridged dictionary that is available to look up the following: *sleazy, cabal, Hobson's choice, narcissism, accolade.*

3. The personnel manager of a large corporation said, "I don't necessarily hire the most intelligent applicant, but I almost always go for the one who knows how to find the necessary information."
    What did he mean? What is the relevance of that personnel manager's statement to this chapter?

TESTS AND EXAMINATIONS: THE BIG SCORE

True Confessions

1. The Scholastic Aptitude Test (S.A.T.) is being given to your class next week. How will you prepare for it? Is it possible to study for a test that measures your intelligence and potential?

   We recommend that you go to a movie, relax with an enjoyable book, and get a good night's sleep before the test. What do you think of this advice?

2. Sir Walter Raleigh wrote, "In examinations, those who do not wish to know, ask questions of those who cannot tell." Does that statement describe the dynamics that exist between your teachers and you? What are the real purposes of tests? Would the education system be improved if examinations were abolished?

3. Henry B. was very confident about his performance on the verbal portion of the Scholastic Aptitude Test because he was especially strong in vocabulary. He was shocked, therefore, when he got a very low score. It seems that the exam asks for *antonyms*, not *synonyms*.

   Has something like this ever happened to you? How can such a disaster be avoided?

The Nature of Tests to Come

As you may already be aware, tests will probably be a part of your life from now on. They have been part of education for many years and are finding their way beyond the classroom, into business, industry, government, and the armed forces. Tests are used to measure fitness for entrance into college, for entrance into professional schools and training programs, and for promotions in business, industry, and the military. These tests will measure aptitude, critical thinking, and knowledge of specific topics. Obviously, doing well on such tests is important.

There is currently some debate over the question of improving one's scores on aptitude tests. Some argue that aptitude is something you have from birth and does not change, and consequently no amount of effort or practice will change one's score on aptitude tests. Others maintain that study and practice can improve scores. Since there is room for doubt that one's aptitude is a measurable constant, it seems reasonable to try to improve as much as one can.

Most general aptitude tests ask questions that test your knowledge of words and your ability to see logical relationships. Perhaps the best way to improve your skills for this kind of test is to increase the size of your vocabulary (etymology is helpful here) by studying words, how they are used, and what they mean. There are also several practice books available to help you study for these tests; usually, the titles of these books will name the test they help you prepare for.

Tests of specific aptitudes are easier to prepare for; merely study the areas being covered in the tests. Review your knowledge of mathematics if you are taking a mathematics test, or mechanics if you are taking a mechanical aptitude test, and so on. It pays to be prepared.

Students bound for college will face scholastic aptitude tests. The tests are divided into two categories: (1) verbal, which tests your ability to deal with reading subjects; and (2) mathematical, which indicates your skill in dealing with numbers. Since it has been proved that success in learning depends more and more upon the ability to read with understanding, comprehension plays a large part in the verbal test. The mathematics test attempts to measure your ability to apply given concepts to new situations, that is, your ability to reason. The best preparation for aptitude tests is a background of vocabulary interest, wide reading, and practice in clear thinking.

College entrance achievement tests, which are given on specific subject material, lend themselves to a certain amount of preparation. Sample achievement tests are available in many subjects; you should take them. If possible you should take achievement tests in your best subjects. Many colleges require achievement tests in English and mathematics, plus one other. Many also require a writing sample in the form of an essay. If you have mastered the art of dealing with essay questions on your school subjects, and can handle the mechanics and diction of good composition, the writing sample should not prove difficult.

Attitude: The First Step

Dr. Francis P. Robinson in his book, *Effective Study*, poses this question: "Did you ever thank a teacher for giving an examination?" At first glance you are not likely to find much in your thinking that would help generate an affirmative answer. The teacher does spend much time preparing the test questions; after you have taken the examination, the teacher spends many hours carefully evaluating your paper. Mistakes are marked so that when your paper is returned you can go over them and perhaps write in corrections so you will not make the same mistakes again.

Do you, like many of your fellow students, consider the test or examination as a personal battle which the teacher wages in an attempt to defeat you, or as a contest in which one tries to outwit the other? If this is your attitude toward tests and examinations, you probably do one of two things when the teacher returns your paper to you. One, you throw it away without bothering to do more than glance through it to see where points were taken off; or two, without checking an incomplete answer against the facts as studied, you approach the teacher and demand to know why points were taken off. This is the most negative of approaches. The difference in attitude can be seen in the difference between two questions: "Why did you take off points on this question?" and "What should I have included which I did not?"

Another attitude that you should avoid is that of fear. Fear of taking tests and examinations results in tension and disturbed thinking, which produce blind spots (not being able to remember answers that you knew ten minutes before the test) and careless mistakes. This fear also keeps people from venturing into new areas in life. They may visualize the new method, the better tool, or the strong bridge, but they hesitate until someone else realizes their dreams.

Fear prevents success on tests and examinations because fear conditions the mind for failure. Students who are afraid start in a state of confusion and disorder; thus they throw away the advantages they have accumulated by preparation. Students who approach tests and examinations with fear are almost always characterized by the following: (1) Their mark is considerably lower than their daily recitation marks, sometimes as much as twenty points lower. (2) They complain about the teacher—insufficient explanation, lack of detailed review, etc. (3) They find fault with the test material—too long, not the type of questions expected and studied for, didn't understand the wording of questions, read the word *muckrakers* instead of *mugwumps* and missed the whole point. (4) Their preparation consists of a frantic last-ditch effort, loss of sleep almost to the point of total exhaustion, and often loss of important notes or review material just when they were needed most. (5) Fear compels these students to study for the test with another student. Invariably they choose a study companion who has the same attitude of fear and whose knowledge of the subject is only equal to, or perhaps less than, their own.

If you recognize two or more of these characteristics as behavior patterns which you practice at test and examination time, you should change your attitude as quickly as possible. To continue them is to subject yourself to a climate of tension and fear and to condition yourself for defeat.

A third attitude is wholly positive. It is the attitude of challenge, self-confidence, and content-reliability. Students who accept a test as a challenge to show the teacher the extent of their knowledge of the subject and to improve their grades are stimulated. This stimulation produces the energy needed to think clearly and to act with precision over a longer period of concentration than the daily recitation requires. The attitude of challenge is reflected by enterprising rather than burdensome preparation, and self-confidence develops from this adequate preparation. There is no room for tension and fear. Even a questionable answer is approached by a calculated reliability that a worthwhile answer, although perhaps only partially correct, can be worked out. This attitude requires the relationship between student and teacher, and question and answer, always to be one of cooperative production rather than competitive destruction.

Learning from Tests

Tests provide opportunities both for your teachers to evaluate your knowledge and skills, and for you to learn. Many students think only of the first aspect of testing and never realize the value tests have in helping them learn.

From tests you can learn what your weaknesses are in a subject and take steps to correct them. Do you make errors in reading questions? Take the time to be more careful in reading. Do you find the questions ask about things you didn't think were important? You may overcome this problem with practice in asking yourself questions about topics, and in making your questions similar to the ones your teacher asks. Do you find your notes do not contain information on which you were tested? Be more alert for key ideas in class—learn from the questions on tests what kind of information your teacher considers important. Make sure that you have that kind of information in your notes. Do you find that your teacher reviewed material for the test but that you did not pay attention? Help yourself by active listening, especially in the time just before a test.

All of these suggestions for learning from tests require that you review your tests when your teacher hands them back. It is a foolish student who discards a test in anger and does not try to learn from his mistakes.

Tests will also give you practice in writing. You will gain practice in organizing essays, in deciding the importance of ideas, and in expressing ideas. To improve your performance in these writing skills, learn from your mistakes. Pay attention to what your teacher writes about your essays and strive to avoid repeating those kinds of mistakes.

Reviewing for Tests and Examinations

The most successful review is the one that starts with the second assignment at the beginning of the term and continues as a part of daily preparation throughout the course. Such a review should include a well-organized notebook, a basic vocabulary for the course, important class notes, all weekly and monthly test questions, and a well-marked textbook, indicating the material designated important during the course. In addition, a mental blueprint should be woven into the material, uniting the parts of the subject into a unified whole.

This procedure cannot be stressed too strongly; the student who fails to follow it usually faces an impossible task a week or two before the examination. We all know how complex and difficult it is to learn even a small amount of material thoroughly; thus, the person who attempts a whole term's work in a week is playing a silly, losing game. If your continuous review is carried out from week to week, preparing for a weekly quiz or a monthly test should require no more time than a regular daily assignment; an hour test should not demand more than two hours of review. Your test review should deal largely with recitation rather than rereading. Check main topics for recall; where main headings draw a blank, do a limited amount of rereading. This, plus careful attention to important questions and hints given by the teacher, should complete your quiz and test preparation. Therefore, suggestions for review which follow are directed mainly toward the final examination. Several of the practices can be adapted for use in preparing for smaller tests.

Examinations demand primarily the recall of large amounts of information. The objective examination requires only recall; the essay examination demands recall plus organization and amplification. Since effective recall depends upon study distributed over a long period of time, even your immediate review for an examination should be divided into hourly periods of study which start ten days or two weeks before the examination. Review should never be started later than a week before the exam. Five one-hour review periods spread over five days are far more beneficial than ten hours of attempted study the day before the examination.

A ten-hour session or a five-hour ordeal the day before the examination, or an all-night period of mental exhaustion and confusion, cannot be considered review. It can only be described as a short-sighted, superficial, and futile struggle to cram a great deal of information into one's mind. At most, cramming provides a smattering of information for short-term use only. The information slips away quickly, usually even before the examination can be finished. Its chief function is to overlay what you have learned during the term with confusion. It is far better to read a good book, go to a movie, get a good night's sleep, and appear at the exam with a fresh clean look.

Pages could be written on the disastrous effects of cramming; the case histories of its ill results and failure would fill volumes. Let us leave its senselessness and learn ways to make a review less a period of self-torture and more a period of profitable study.

Suggestions for Successful Review

1. Learn to select what is most important to learn. General principles, formulas and experimental conclusions, vocabularies and rules, historical sequences and literary types, and theories and facts are some of the important items in your courses. Be sure to differentiate between opinion and fact. Pay particular attention to material that is emphasized by boldface type, questions, or repeated in summary paragraphs.

2. Listen with such precision during the two weeks before the examination that you miss nothing that is said in class. Even though the teacher may be continuing with new material, there are signs to indicate that important items for review are being made available to you. Listen for such statements as: "In October we studied a case not unlike this one. Remember why it was considered so important." "This is the eighth essential principle we have studied this term. They are all important to an understanding of the course." Most teachers refer in one way or another to almost everything you will see on the examination. Listen for it.

    It is also important to keep your eyes open. Remember the story of the teacher who filled the blackboard with French and English sentences, vocabulary words, rules, etc., a week before examination time. Nothing was said to explain why all this had been written there, and no one asked. When the students saw the examination, the truth was self-evident. The examination had been on the blackboard for a whole week. Two students smiled and began writing perfect papers; they had seen.

The others had looked too, but had seen nothing; they each got about their expected grade.

3. Review by using questions to predict questions. When you have found what you consider important, turn it into a question, or ask yourself how it could be made into a question. This requires discipline, for many students choose the easy method of forming only questions which they know they can answer. However, the easy questions are never the only ones asked on examinations. Be honest; accept the hard ones and prepare answers. Good students can predict close to 90% of an examination.

Do not confuse prediction that results from thorough study with a guessing game. It does not mean simply trying to outguess the teacher, and doing only spot studying. This is usually fatal. You have often heard the victim lament, "I thought he was going to ask _____, but he didn't, so I had to blank four whole questions."

4. Review by reorganizing your course material. Where possible, reduce the subject matter to easily remembered divisions. In mathematics these divisions may be definitions, word problems, theorems, formulas, and general concepts. In history they may be biography, chronology, reform movements (radical), reform movements (conservative), domestic wars, foreign wars, economic problems, civic problems, and religious problems. This is one of the most profitable of all review procedures. At first glance it may appear to hinder unity and continuity of the subject. However, it does just the opposite; it binds the parts of the course into a more workable and understandable unit.

5. Review by changing your point of view. If you have dealt with a subject during the term from the point of view of memorization to receive a credit only, change your point of view to that of application for understanding. The first point of view is a deterrent to successful

study; the second is one of study's greatest psychological aids. And unless your mind is prepared, there can be no profitable review.

Change your point of view from that of observer to participant. If you are reviewing history, put yourself into character. Accept a role—not the king, the general, or the hero—through which you can get a comprehensive feeling for the people you are studying. Be a slave, a common soldier, a person in the street. If you are reviewing a foreign language, imagine that in six weeks you will be allowed to use only this language.

Reviewing by changing your point of view can be an exciting game. Use your imagination and find new approaches to all your subjects.

6. Make question "terminology" and question "reading" a part of your review. Although certain words appear in question after question, these key words often mean different things to different teachers. You must know what the teacher expects when the question says *explain, evaluate, state, relate, illustrate, enumerate, describe, interpret, define, diagram, compare, contrast, compare and contrast.* Practice reading chapter-end questions to understand exactly what a question asks for. Note the characteristics of questions that pertain to different subjects. Some subjects lend themselves to specifics; questions in other subjects are very general. Question "knowledge" should be an important part of any review.

Taking Tests and Examinations

Tests and examinations are generally of two kinds: objective and subjective. Objective, or short-answer, tests require you to recognize correct answers among incorrect ones, or true statements set beside false ones. Objective tests also measure your ability to recall details. Objective questions are usually one of the following types: (1) Recall (filling in blanks): Joseph Conrad was born in _____ and spent his early years _____. (2) Recognition (multiple choice): Gandhi learned of civil disobedience from (a) Emerson (b) Gladstone (c) Lincoln (d) Marx (e) Thoreau. Ans. (   ). True or False questions are also considered recognition questions: Mockingbirds belong to the mimic family. (T) Mockingbirds belong to the sparrow family. (F) A third type of recognition question is the matching question. For example, write the number of the phrase which fits the character in the space provided:

1.	Founder of Hebrew Nation	2	Lincoln
2.	The Great Emancipator	1	Moses
3.	Apostle of Peace	4	Gladstone
4.	Three times Prime Minister	5	Einstein
5.	Scientist and Philosopher	3	Woodrow Wilson

Here are some things that you should consider in approaching objective examinations:

1. Pay particular attention to mechanical instructions; that is, instructions that tell you *where* and *how* to answer questions. Wrong position may result in wrong answers; in any case, answering in ways other than that required may cause the teacher difficulty in grading your paper. Some teachers take off points when instructions are not followed.

2. Make a quick survey of the whole test before writing any answer. Get an overview to help you determine how quickly you will need to work.

3. The questions are usually numerous; sometimes you do not have to answer all of them. Always answer the questions that you know first and come back to any that you wish to spend time on.

4. Read certain types of objective questions (particularly True-False) so that you observe all qualifying words. These words—*usually, always, most, never, some*—give insight into when and under what conditions a

statement is or is not correct. Modifiers play their most important role in True-False questions.

5. All objective questions require correct reading. Don't let premeditated opinion cause you to read into the question a word that is not there. This results in wrong answers, and after the examination you are heard to say, "But I thought the question was."

6. Do not change answers too quickly as you check your examination before turning it in. Your first answer might be more reliable unless you are absolutely sure you have made a mistake. If there is any doubt, leave the first answer.

7. Do not think that neatness and order can be ignored on objective examinations. Words and numbers can be written sloppily or neatly. Neatness begins with the first blank you fill and ends with the way you sign your name.

The second kind of test, the subjective, demands more of the student in both recalling and organizing subject matter. These are usually called "essay" tests; they may be short-answer questions (a paragraph) or discussion questions (a lengthy essay which measures the student's entire scope of knowledge on a particular part of the course). The word "subjective" implies that this kind of examination is more personal than the objective test. It provides students with a greater opportunity to show the extent of their preparation. It also provides the teacher with a chance to make more personal judgments in evaluating the paper. For this reason you should think in terms of what judgment you would make of your answers if you were the teacher.

Essay examinations measure your ability to recall what you have learned, organize it intelligently, and express it clearly and with meaningful interpretation, selection, or application, depending upon what is asked for. The first and most important thing to remember about essay examination questions is that there is no such thing as a *general answer*.

You can write successful essay examinations by practicing a few *must* requirements:

1. Read through all the essay questions before you start to write and allot time to each question. Divide the time available for the test according to the importance of the questions. A question that is worth 25 percent of the test should get 25 percent of the available time.

2. Read the question to determine exactly what it asks you to do and what instructions are included for doing it. If the question asks for Alexander's spiritual legacy, it is a waste of time to describe the physical legacy (army, devoted generals, etc.) he received from his father. As in objective questions, qualifying words give the question its explicit meaning. Yet some students misread questions. The student who reads *conservationists* instead of *conservatives* may write a beautiful answer, but he will get no credit; he answered a question that wasn't asked. The qualifying words of a question are really the directions for answering it. A record of careless mistakes on tests and examinations made by students at Kent School over a five-year period showed that carelessness in reading the question was responsible for 64 percent of all careless mistakes.

3. Read the first question you are going to answer and write a brief outline of your major points in the margin. Think for a minute or two about your answer to check the arrangement of ideas. Make sure your answer includes all important ideas. THINKING BEFORE WRITING will improve your essays as nothing else will.

4. As you write, restate the question if you can, but at least make the subject of the question the subject of your answer. Never start an answer with a pronoun without an antecedent. Two such beginnings, fatal to a good mark but often used, are: "It is when" and "It is because." Always make the subject of the question the subject of your answer. As you read the question

for the second time you must constantly watch for anything that will give your answer an element of vagueness.

5. As you write your answer keep in mind the teacher's preference for style of presentation, use of illustration to show understanding, and elements of a model answer. If the teacher has complimented you on earlier test papers for the way you handled an answer, try to apply this method to as many questions as possible. Ask yourself the question, "What is the teacher's aim in this particular question?" Make your paper easy to mark. Use signal words and numerals to introduce important facts and series. Number questions to the left of the red margin and skip one or two lines between answers. Remember that the neatly written paper has fewer mistakes and is easier for the teacher to mark.

6. Concentrate on one question at a time, and use a mental system of numbering important points in your answer. Students often "overwrite" or "write away from" questions because they jump ahead and are thinking of a question to come. The teacher has not asked questions that require repeating subject matter, so be careful to keep all answers within the limits set by the questions. An excellent method for avoiding generalizations and worthless "padding" is to mentally number important points as you write them down. Illustrations, specific elaboration, important facts, and explanations to clarify your understanding of a definition or event are all necessary parts of a good essay answer. If you number important items mentally as you write, you will see the difference between what has value (and will add to your mark) and what is worthless.

7. Check over the completed examination paper before you turn it in. You should reserve ten minutes of each examination hour for checking after you have completed the writing. Check for mechanical errors and obvious factual mistakes such as wrong words, incorrect conclusions, transposed characters, etc. As with ob-

jective tests, do not change anything in an answer unless you are absolutely sure it is wrong. Rely on your first impression.

8. You can learn much about writing better examinations and using better methods of study by going over the graded paper after it has been returned. By checking against your book you can see what you omitted that the teacher considered important or how you misinterpreted the qualifying word in a question. If you note such errors carefully, you will not repeat them on the next test.

Summary of Rules for Reviewing For and Taking Tests and Examinations

1. Review by selecting the important subject matter; concentrate on it rather than on the trivial and incidental.

2. Review by listening for hints and helps given by the teacher just prior to the test.

3. Review by predicting questions for the test. Think how questions can be asked on specific subject matter.

4. Review by reorganizing the subject matter into logical divisions. Keep a sense of unity by being aware of relationships among parts.

5. Review by changing your point of view. Let your imagination add interest to the subject.

6. Review by knowing what "question words" mean. Learn what your teacher expects when certain key words are used.

7. When you take the test or examination read all questions and instructions carefully and repeatedly until

you understand exactly what the answer and the presentation of the answer require.

8. Know the general implications of key and qualifying words in both objective and essay questions. Do not, under any circumstances, make an exception for what the qualifying word asks for.

9. On objective tests give the precise answer; on essay tests give the complete answer. Always remember that quantity without quality will not get a good grade.

10. Observe all rules of neatness, mechanics, and clarity. The attractive paper that is easy to read gets the better grade.

11. Check your paper carefully before you turn it in. Unless you are absolutely sure you have made a mistake, do not change your answers. The first impression, as psychological tests have shown, is more reliable.

12. Improve all future test and examination grades by carefully checking all returned papers. Note your errors and shortcomings so you will not repeat them on the next test.

Looking Back

1. What do teachers and test makers mean when they ask you to do the following?
    a. Evaluate
    b. Describe
    c. Compare and contrast

2. Some baseball batters are "guess hitters." They guess at the kind of pitch that will be thrown to them (fast ball, curve, slider, change of pace) and then swing. Should you guess about test questions your teacher is likely to ask and prepare for them exclusively?

Do you study with a friend who knows more or less than you do? What are the advantages and disadvantages of studying for a test with a friend?

3. One proven tip for test takers is to check their paper over thoroughly before submitting it to the teacher. List three additional tips you found in this chapter. What suggestion, if any, could you make that was not mentioned in this chapter?

MOTIVATION: EACH MUST FIND IT FOR ONESELF

The Reach and the Grasp

"Ah, but a man's reach should exceed his grasp, Or what's a heaven for?" Thus wrote Robert Browning in his poem, "Andrea del Sarto," in 1855. Although what is within one's reach today has multiplied beyong the vaguest dream of anyone living in Browning's day, it is still a part of natural law that unless one's dreams exceed what one is momentarily capable of grasping, one stops learning. One's life becomes mere survival; finally one is pushed off the stage by a better actor who has developed a greater capacity to reach for dreams. William Golding makes this point in an exciting book entitled *The Inheritors*, in which he describes how slow-witted Neanderthal man was replaced by a person capable of greater vision—Cro-Magnon man.

"But what has this to do with me?" you ask. Beginning with your endowments and the gifts that grow from these endowments, we have encompassed all of the best study methods and practices. They are within both your grasp and your reach to improve your grades. However, if you are really going to succeed, you must extend the demands you make upon these learning processes to drive you from what you are toward what you can become.

This factor, which determines success or failure both in school and in life, is elusive, difficult to isolate from the whole of one's character, and also impossible to define. It is a combination of interest, ambition, inspiration, moral acceptance of life's importance, a sense of values, and faith in oneself. It is sometimes called by one of the several parts ascribed to it, but generally it is given a name which suggests forward movement and the rhythm of a firm quick step—*motivation*.

The power of motivation lies in striving to be the best, not in merely appearing so. Without motivation, people atrophy and civilizations decline. You can ponder forever what makes one person succeed and another fail. But if you were asked why a great civilization declines, you might answer, "A great civilization declines not because geography changes but because people's minds change." People become satisfied and cease to be excited about learning. Civilization declines when people do not want to do and to know; when work becomes drudgery and love of learning is replaced by resentment and impatience; when the aim of learning becomes social status rather than truth and ennoblement.

What do we really know of this moving purpose, motivation, that so profoundly affects people and nations? First, we should remind ourselves that motivation is that which strives for what is excellent. Perhaps we can find how much of the whole concept of motivation is within us by looking at some of its components.

What can all the study methods in the world do for you if you lack interest? No one can be interested for you; your parents cannot wish it upon you; your teachers cannot force it upon you. Interest is the basic obligation that you must carry into each classroom. Interest often transforms subject matter from something very dead into something active and alive. As Jacques Maritain puts it in his book *Education at the Crossroads*,

> What is learned should never be passively received or mechanically received, as dead information which weighs down and dulls the mind. It must rather be transformed by understanding into the very life of the mind, and thus strengthen the latter, as wood

thrown into the fire and transformed into flame makes the fire stronger.[1]

Interest gives work a new dimension. Tom Sawyer discovered it when he had his friends whitewash the fence for him. "Work," he said, "consists of whatever a body is obliged to do, and play consists of whatever a body is not obliged to do." Interest gives obligation the quality and character of privilege. You can use interest to take the feeling of compulsion out of study. Interest will help you do more and better work than is required. The clockwatcher finds the day long and seemingly endless. The interested worker never has all the time he or she wants. Perhaps interest, as a component of motivation, is best summed up by an old axiom that has long hung on the walls of a classroom at Kent School: "If a man does only what is required of him he is a slave, the moment he does more he is a free man."

What of the ingredient of motivation we call ambition? It is far more than simple willingness to receive. Alexander the Great, at the age of twenty, inherited a well-equipped army led by brilliant and devoted generals. If Alexander had been content only to receive, the army would soon have belonged to the generals. Students who have jobs waiting or places in their fathers' companies often feel that school is a waste of time. They wait to take over; then they quickly lose their places to someone who has learned that ambition is a positive, purposeful, creative force.

Ambition, like the other ingredients of motivation, can be measured by the drop or by the barrel. It is within your power to inventory whatever ambition is within you. Only you can add up your resources, color them by bold strokes with the brush of imagination, and hold them before you as a bright picture of your abilities.

It is easy to make a check list of your ambitions concerning your school work. In addition, much that will pertain to your

---

1. Jacques Maritain, *Education at the Crossroads* (New Haven: Yale University Press, 1943), 50.

life's ambitions should be put on your check list while you are still in school: (1) What are my abilities? (2) What will my ambition require of me? (3) What will success mean in the career or job for which I aim? (4) What will defeat mean? (5) Have I put the proper value upon my life and my time? (6) Will my work provide sufficient inspiration and challenge to save me from complacency and stagnation?

We could continue through some explanation of all the components of motivation, but by now you should see what is happening. We have come full circle and are talking about your gifts as described in Chapter 1. Thus, the only way to understand the meaning of motivation is to understand your own gifts and the uses to which they can be put.

Don't stand still if you can walk; don't walk if you can run; don't run if you can fly. There is an old Indian legend of an eaglet that thought it was a prairie chicken and never used its wings. As the story goes, an Indian boy found an eagle's egg and put it in a prairie chicken's nest. The eaglet hatched with the brood of prairie chicks and grew up with them. The changeling eagle, thinking it was a prairie chicken, did what prairie chickens did. It scratched in the dirt for seeds and insects to eat, never flew more than a short distance, and that with an awkward flutter of wings, only a few feet off the ground. After all, that's how prairie chickens were supposed to fly.

Then one day when the eagle was grown, it saw a magnificent bird far above it in the sky. Riding with graceful majesty on the powerful wind currents, it soared with scarcely a beat of its golden wings.

"What a beautiful bird!" said the eagle to one of the prairie chickens. "What is it?"

"That's an eagle, the chief of birds," the prairie chicken replied. "But don't give it a second thought. You could never fly like it."

So the eagle never gave it a second thought, never rose beyond the brief thrashing of wings and the flurry of feathers, and grew old, and died thinking it was a prairie chicken. It's all too easy to go through life thinking we're prairie chickens when we're really eagles.

Motivation—Imperishable

Let us conclude with two true stories to illustrate a fact: if you show concern for both the better self of which you are capable and your gifts through which you can achieve this better self, motivation will take care of itself.

Not all your papers will be returned with honor grades. When you have done your best and still get a low grade, there will be moments of discouragement, doubt, and depression. When this happens, remind yourself of the following story:

The first scene of the story is set in the wilderness of Indiana. A small boy trudges through the winter forest to a one-room school. After six weeks the school closed and the boy suffered the first of many deeply felt disappointments. By the time he was twenty-two, he had wandered as an itinerant worker and was now a partner in a crossroads store at the edge of a frontier village in Illinois. The store failed and he lost every penny he had saved from seven years' hard labor.

The lesson had been expensive, but he felt that he had learned by hard experience. He would not fail again. Two years of struggle provided him with enough funds to enter a second partnership. This time he would succeed. But within two years the second store had failed. The young man's partner drank up the profits. The person to whom the partners sold the store failed to make his payments, and when the entire stock of goods had been sold, disappeared with the receipts. When the former partner died the young man was left with debts which seemed impossible to ever pay off.

Now he asked a friend to help him get a job as a surveyor, and he studied mathematics with the village schoolmaster to prepare himself for the job. After he was appointed to the surveyor's job, he borrowed money to buy instruments and a horse; however, he never had a chance to begin work. Creditors from his mercantile failures seized his possessions and he lost both horse and instruments.

Immediately after this the gods dealt him the cruelest blow of all, convincing him that he had been singled out for pain and failure from birth. His sweetheart, perhaps a deep and enduring love, the like of which he did not experience again, suddenly died. He descended to the depths of despair and gloom, often pondering whether the struggle to live was worth it. Long afterward he wrote, "At this period of my life I never dared to carry a pocketknife, fearing I would destroy myself."

Time passes. The man no longer looks young, although he is not yet forty. After ten years of struggle he has paid off the last of his debts. While he worked to pay them off, he also spent long hours trying to satisfy his insatiable hunger to learn, to be able to put into words what he felt, to understand the feelings of men around him.

Friends began to suggest that this failure might be a success in the most unexpected of places—politics. So they elected him to Congress. He did not succeed; after two short terms he was defeated for reelection. Nine years later his staunch friends determined to nominate him for the U.S. Senate. However, a split developed in the party and he was forced to step aside in favor of a candidate who could win the number of votes for nomination. This too was failure. Two years later, when he did manage to be nominated and run for the Senate, he was soundly defeated. Of this failure he said, "I was down and out of politics at the age of 50." Looking back over thirty years of his life he could not claim a single personal victory.

The motivating forces of gods and men, of fate, of dreams and destiny, are beyond prediction and comprehension. No man knows when he is walking with destiny, and no man was ever less suspecting than this long-time loser. For in the 52nd year of life, in the 32nd year of failure, this man was elected President of the United States. He is usually listed among the half-dozen greatest men who ever lived. His name, of course, is Abraham Lincoln.

Motivation—A Seed Falling Upon Good Ground

The second story is really a continuation of the first. Abraham Lincoln had one thing in common with Anthony La Manna. Anthony was born on April 14; the day on which Lincoln was shot. The years were different, however; Lincoln was shot in 1865 and Anthony La Manna was born in 1888 in the village of Valguarnera Caropepe, amid the stone quarries of Monte Erei.

Anthony La Manna, one of eleven children, entered the quarries as a laborer at the age of twelve. Under the scorching Sicilian sun, amid the deafening ringing of hammers and thunderous thuds and rattles of giant slabs of stone crashing into pits, Anthony La Manna dreamed of nothing beyond the sulphur and rock-salt mines near the sea, where the pay was better. But even these mines seemed far away. They were south over the hills and past the valley through which ran the Assinarus River. Tony could wipe the sweat from his brow and scan the jagged horizon, but the hope of better wages from sulphur or rock-salt mines was far away—perhaps too far.

Few ever went from the quarries. The pattern of trudging up the mountain at sunrise and back down at sunset, with an occasional goatherd to offer news from beyond the hills, became for most the center and circumference of a world.

Anthony La Manna, reading the history of his island with his fifth-grade education, and listening to his elders talk, felt that change was against the natural order of things. Sicily, he thought, had really not changed much in the 2315 years since Nicias and the Athenian army had been destroyed on the banks of the Assinarus River in 415 B.C. The Athenians who were defeated in battle were enslaved in the quarries, where they were scorched by the sun and where they died. Anthony La Manna had also seen men die in the quarries.

When Tony La Manna was sixteen, he followed the valley and the river down to the sea. In the Gulf of Gela a ship was loading goods to carry to America, and Anthony La Manna "hired on."

There were times in America when Anthony would have given much to be back on the road which led homeward from the quarry, where the friendly voice of the goatherd broke the loneliness. But his four years in the quarries had given him much skill with a chisel and a hammer on stone; after a short time of digging ditches in the swamps of New Jersey, he became a stonecutter's apprentice in Washington, D.C.

Sixteen years in America, aged thirty-two, proud of the only diploma he ever dreamed of possessing—a stonecutter's union card—he is chosen to carve the Gettysburg Address on the Lincoln Memorial. Day after day, as he worked high on the scaffold, he studied the countenance on the gigantic statue. The sad, tired man, who had begun life in surroundings as humble as those of Tony La Manna, had become a lawyer, and a President. He had saved his country in its most trying hour and had given voice to the immortal words that a Sicilian immigrant boy was now writing in stone to be "forever enshrined" in the hearts of men.

One day at lunch time, as Tony La Manna sat on the end of the high scaffold looking into the middle section of the great monument, where sat the rail splitter from the wilderness of Illinois, the stone splitter from Monte Erei made a sudden decision—Anthony La Manna could make something more of himself. He would become a lawyer. On a piece of planking he wrote "Anthony LaManna" and under his name "Attorney at Law." At the end of the day he brought the piece of board down from the scaffold. His friends laughed—"Another Aba Lincoln mayba. Tony, you looka too much at the statue."

It's a long way from a noisy fifth grade class in the little stuc-coed school in Caropepe, Sicily, to the National Law Center at George Washington University in Washington, D.C. After ten hours on a scaffold with chisel and hammer, there was night school—"Engulesh, how you say in Engulesh! Noun, verb, what for pronoun, adjudgtive?" And in his canvas bag with chis-els, hammer, and salami sandwiches, Tony La Manna carried books. He would hurry through his lunch and begin to read. His friends would laugh, as long before Lincoln's rail-splitting com-panions had laughed at him, as he sat on a stump with a book in one hand and a slab of salt pork between two chunks of corn-bread in the other.

Finally Anthony La Manna was admitted to law school. But World War I came, and he went away to fight for democracy and the right to be free and learn and become something in Amer-ica. When he came back he earned an LL.B. and an LL.M. in rapid succession.

For nearly forty years he was a successful lawyer in both New York and Washington, and was special counselor to the Vet-eran's Administration for thirty-two years. When I asked him if I could tell his story to illustrate the meaning of motivation, he thought I should find a better example. When I asked him to describe what he considered motivation, he said, "Impossible, for each man must discover and define it for himself."

So ends the story, the chapter, and this book. What is moti-vation and from whence does it come? The answer is as difficult to describe as trying to tell the direction of the wind by hearing it move through far-off hills at night. Unless you find your own answer to what motivation is, you will never know. If you have it, you will know; if you do not have it, those around you will know.

You can escape neither time nor history. Unless you use the gifts you have been given, time will close many doors which open on long corridors of opportunity through which you will never be permitted to walk. As you turn your back on the closed doors to walk in the tracks you have already made, you will find history gazing upon you, holding you accountable for misappropriation.

"Of what?" you demand.

"Of your talents," answers history.